The Proper Care of
ROTTWEILERS

TW-142

Opposite: *Eight-week-old Rodsden's Patrina owned by Rodsden's Rotweilers, reg.*

Distributed in the UNITED STATES to the Pet Trade by T.F.H. Publications, Inc., One T.F.H. Plaza, Neptune City, NJ 07753; distributed in the UNITED STATES to the Bookstore and Library Trade by National Book Network, Inc. 4720 Boston Way, Lanham MD 20706; in CANADA to the Pet Trade by H & L Pet Supplies Inc., 27 Kingston Crescent, Kitchener, Ontario N2B 2T6; Rolf C. Hagen Ltd., 3225 Sartelon Street, Montreal 382 Quebec; in CANADA to the Book Trade by Macmillan of Canada (A Division of Canada Publishing Corporation), 164 Commander Boulevard, Agincourt, Ontario M1S 3C7; in ENGLAND by T.F.H. Publications, PO Box 15, Waterlooville PO7 6BQ; in AUSTRALIA AND THE SOUTH PACIFIC by T.F.H. (Australia), Pty. Ltd., Box 149, Brookvale 2100 N.S.W., Australia; in NEW ZEALAND by Brooklands Aquarium Ltd., 5 McGiven Drive, New Plymouth, RD1 New Zealand; in the PHILIPPINES by Bio-Research, 5 Lippay Street, San Lorenzo Village, Makati, Rizal; in SOUTH AFRICA by Multipet Pty. Ltd., P.O. Box 35347, Northway, 4065, South Africa. Published by T.F.H. Publications, Inc. Manufactured in the United States of America by T.F.H. Publications, Inc.

The Proper Care of
ROTTWEILERS

Joan R. Klem and
Susan C. Rademacher

Dutch Ch. Nadja v t Straotje, IPO I owned by T. Emmers.

Contents

Rodsden's Wilhelmina bred by Rodsden's Rottweilers, reg.

Introduction

Legend has it that the origin of the Rottweiler goes back to the molossus dogs of antiquity—those stalwart mastiff-type dogs which accompanied Hannibal over the Alps into what is now Europe. There, in local pockets of civilization, various breeds developed from

Worldsiegerin Boedy v t Straotje owned by the author, imported by Rodsden's Rottweilers, reg.

Ch. Bruin v Hohenzollern, CDX, circa 1960s, pulling a Conestoga wagon.

this common stem. In Switzerland, for example, the Grosser Schweitzer Sennenhund came into being, in England the English Mastiff, and under the red tiled roofs of the medieval German town of Rottweil, located on the Necker River, a remarkable breed evolved into what we now know as the Rottweiler.

Referred to as the Butcher's dog, or Metzgerhund, this predecessor to our modern Rottweiler served his master by herding cattle to market, guarding his master's purse, and pulling the butchers' carts. All this required a dog of endurance, great strength, and loyalty, but most importantly, an animal capable of executing a variety of tasks.

The ability of the Rottweiler to adapt over the centuries to whatever uses man found for him is why we find that today, of all the mastiff-type breeds in the world, the Rottweiler is the most popular.

At the beginning of the 20th century the modern Rottweiler emerged after the Allegemeiner Deutschen Rottweiler Klub (ADRK) in Germany published its first stud book in 1924. Medium large, black and tan, and with an indomitable

The Rottweiler's original purpose was as a drover dog for cattle and the breed can still perform that job today.

personality, the Rottweiler found his niche as a superb police and military dog. Throughout this century the ADRK has nurtured, refined, and protected the Rottweiler through its breeders' adherence to strict breeding rules. These dedicated German breeders passed on a marvelous and remarkable "product" to the fanciers around the world. No country has better appreciated, or more successfully "marketed", the Rottweiler than the United States.

In 1931 the first Rottweiler appeared in the American Kennel Club's (AKC)

stud book. In 1992 the AKC registered over 70,000 Rottweilers—making the Rottweiler the second most popular breed in the United States, having

International and Dutch Ch. Arko v d Runderkraal, SchH III owned by J. Geerts.

Retriever standing in the way of the Rottweiler's ascent to the number one spot.

Both the Cocker and Lab are members of the Sporting Group whose breeds are known for their friendly and passive temperaments. That the Rottweiler, whose strength, intelligence, and guarding instincts are so well pronounced, finds itself in this popularity race with these soft-spirited sporting dogs is a cause for alarm. For while it seems like everybody now has a Rottweiler, in truth, the Rottweiler is certainly not suitable for everyone!

passed up the Cocker Spaniel, and with only the Labrador

Ch. Trollegen's Frodo, CD owned by M. Wilkinson.

Standard for the Rottweiler

To purchase a Rottweiler, no less to breed a Rottweiler, you must know precisely what a good Rottweiler looks like. Every registering organization, such as

Ch. Eppo v d Keizerslanden, CDX, Canadian CD, BH is in the Medallion Rottweiler Club Hall of Fame as well as being an American Rottweiler Club Gold Producer. Owner, Rodsden's Rottweilers, reg.

An eight-week-old Rottweiler puppy should be curious and adventuresome. This is Ch. Rodsden's Parry v Gunter, A/C CD, TD, CGC, HIC in his younger days. Owned, handled, and trained by Howard Bernier.

the American Kennel Club or the Kennel Club of England, adopts an official standard for the breed, a description of what the *ideal* representative of the breed should look like.

Standards, like purebred dogs for the most part, are manmade and man-remade, which is to say they change over time. These "word pictures" are subject not only to change but also to interpretation. In a perfect world, every breeder is striving for the flawless dog, which is identical in every way to the next breeder's flawless dog, which is identical in every way to the next breeder's flawless dog. In reality, however, the flawless dog doesn't exist, never has and never will. Nonetheless, breeders strive to create that "perfect specimen" and smart owners strive to find that "perfect puppy."

Read the following breed standard carefully and repeatedly. Envision every part of the dog and ask an experienced breeder or exhibitor about anything you don't

Before you purchase a Rottweiler, you should be familiar with what a good Rottweiler looks like.

understand completely.

When buying a puppy, you should know what to look for and NOT to look for. Pay close attention to disqualifications and faults. When considering gait, remember that your puppy is but a "toddler;" instead observe the movement of the parents or other relatives. Structure as well as movement are passed along from

Observe the parents of the pup you are considering. Structure as well as temperament are passed along from generation to generation. This is Dagmar and her five-week-old daughter. Owner, Rodsden's Rottweilers, reg.

parent to offspring.

AKC STANDARD FOR THE ROTTWEILER

General Appearance—The ideal Rottweiler is a medium large, robust and powerful dog, black with clearly defined rust markings. His compact and substantial build denotes great strength, agility and endurance. Dogs are characteristically more massive throughout with larger frame and heavier bone than bitches. Bitches are distinctly feminine, but without weakness of substance or structure.

Size, Proportion, Substance—Dogs - 24 inches to 27 inches.

Head study of Ch. Wasatch Rock v h Brabantpark, CDX, TD owned by Sue Rademacher.

Bitches - 22 inches to 25 inches, with preferred size being mid-range of each sex. Correct proportion is of primary importance, as long as size is within the standard's range. The length of body, from prosternum to the rear most projection of the rump, is slightly longer than the height of the dog at the withers, the most desirable proportion of the height to length being 9 to 10. The Rottweiler is neither coarse nor shelly. Depth of chest is approximately 50 percent of the height of the dog. His bone and muscle mass must be sufficient to balance his frame, giving a compact and very powerful

The Rottweiler has a compact and very powerful appearance.

The Rottweilers expression is noble, alert and self-assured. This is Harbor v d Runderkraal owned by J. Geerts.

appearance. *Serious Faults* — Lack of proportion, undersized, oversized, reversal of sex characteristics (bitchy dogs, doggy bitches).

Head—Of medium length, broad between the ears; forehead line seen in profile is moderately arched; zygomatic arch and stop well developed with strong broad upper and lower jaws. The desired ratio of backskull to muzzle is 3 to 2. Forehead is preferred dry; however, some wrinkling may occur when the dog is alert. **Expression** is noble, alert, and self-assured. **Eyes** of medium size, almond shaped with well fitting lids, moderately deep-set, neither protruding nor receding. The desired color is a uniform dark brown. *Serious Faults*—Yellow (bird of prey) eyes, eyes of different color or size, hairless eye rim. *Disqualifications*—Entropion. Ectropion. **Ears** of medium size, pendant, triangular in shape; when carried alertly the ears are level with the top of the skull and appear to broaden it. Ears are to be set well apart, hanging forward with the inner edge lying tightly against the head and terminating at approximately mid-cheek. *Serious Faults*—Improper carriage (creased, folded or held away from the cheek/head). **Muzzle**—Bridge is straight, broad at base with slight tapering towards tip. The end of the muzzle is broad rather than round and always black; corners closed; inner mouth pigment is

A/C and International Ch. Barto v t Straotje, IPO III, A/C TD owned by Frank Fiorella.

This nine-month-old Rottweiler already possesses the powerful, well-muscled neck called for in the breed standard.

22 lower), strong, correctly placed, meeting in a scissors bite - lower incisors touching inside of upper incisors. *Serious Faults*—Level bite; any missing tooth. *Disqualifications*— Overshot, undershot (when incisors do not touch or mesh); wry mouth; two or more missing teeth.

Neck, Topline, Body—*Neck*— Powerful, well muscled, moderately long, slightly arched and without loose skin. **Topline**— The back is firm and level, extending in a straight line from behind the withers to the croup. The back remains horizontal to

preferred dark. *Serious Faults*—Total lack of mouth pigment (pink mouth). **Bite and dentition**—Teeth 42 in number (20 upper,

the ground while the dog is moving or standing. ***Body***— The chest is roomy, broad and deep, reaching to elbow, with well pronounced forechest and well spring, oval ribs. Back is straight and strong. Loin is short, deep and well muscled. Croup is broad, of medium length and only slightly sloping. Underline of a mature Rottweiler has a slight tuck-up. Males must have two normal testicles properly descended into the scrotum.

The Rottweiler's tail should be docked short and close to the body. This is Ch. Quinto v h Brabantpark, CD owned by Linda Wright and Shirley Werner.

Disqualification—Unilateral cryptorchid or cryptorchid males. **Tail**—Tail docked short, close to body, leaving one or two tail vertebrae. The set of the tail is more important than length. Properly set, it gives an impression of elongation of the topline; carried slightly above horizontal when the dog is excited or moving.

Ch. Gundi v Reichenbachle owned by Rodsden's Rottweilers, reg.

Forequarters—Shoulder blade is long and well laid back. Upper arm equal in length to shoulder blade, set so elbows are well under body. Distance from withers to elbow and elbow to groin is equal. Legs are strongly developed with straight, heavy bone, not set close together. Pasterns are strong, springy and almost perpendicular to the ground. Feet are round, compact with well arched toes, turning neither in nor out. Pads are thick and hard. Nails short, strong and black. Dewclaws may be removed.

Hindquarters— Angulation of hindquarters balances that of forequarters. Upper thigh is fairly long, very broad and well muscled. Stifle joint is well tuned. Lower thigh is long, broad and powerful with extensive muscling

Ch. Rodsden's Quito of Wylan, CDX, TDX, BH, SchH III, IPO III, FH, CGC, HIC—"the complete Rottweiler"—owned and trained by Ron Maloney and co-owned by Sue Rademacher.

leading into a strong hock joint. Rear pasterns are nearly perpendicular to the ground. Viewed from the rear, hind legs are straight, strong and wide enough apart to fit with a properly built body. Feet are somewhat longer than the front

The Rottweiler has a double coat—a harsh, straight, short outer coat and a soft undercoat. During the winter months the undercoat is thicker. Ch. Wasatch v h Brabantpark CDX, TD owned by Sue Rademacher.

The Rottweiler is always black with tan to mahogany markings.

feet, turning neither in nor out, equally compact with well arched toes. Pads are thick and hard. Nails short, strong and black. Dewclaws must be removed.

Coat— Outer coat is straight, coarse, dense, of medium length and lying flat. Undercoat should be present on neck and thighs, but the amount is influenced by climatic conditions. Undercoat should not show through outer coat. The coat is shortest on head, ears and legs, longest on breeching. The Rottweiler is to be exhibited in the natural condition with no trimming.

Fault— Wavy coat.
Serious Faults—
Open, excessively
short, or curly coat;
total lack of
undercoat; any
trimming that alters
the length of the
natural coat.
Disqualification—
Long coat.

Color— Always
black with rust to
mahogany markings.
The demarcation
between black and
rust is to be clearly
defined. The
markings should be
located as follows: a
spot over each eye;
on cheeks; as a strip
around each side of
muzzle, but not on
the bridge of the
nose; on throat;
triangular mark on
both sides of

prosternum; on
forelegs from carpus
downward to the
toes; on inside of rear

legs showing down the front of the stifle and broadening out to front of rear legs from hock to toes, but not completely eliminating black from rear of pasterns; under tail; black penciling on toes. The undercoat is gray, tan, or black. Quantity and location of rust markings is important and should not exceed ten percent of body color. *Serious Faults*— Straw colored, excessive, insufficient or sooty markings; rust marking other than described above; white marking any place on dog (a few rust or white hairs do not constitute a marking).

A/C Ch. Rodsden's Elko Kastanienbaum, CDX, TD, Can. CD, MRC Hall of Fame, ARC Gold Producer owned by Gary Klem.

Disqualifications— Any base color other than black; absence of all markings.

Gait—The Rottweiler is a trotter. His movement should be balanced, harmonious, sure, powerful and unhindered, with strong forereach and a powerful rear drive. The motion is effortless, efficient and ground-covering.

The Rottweiler's movement should be balanced, harmonious, sure, powerful and unhindered, with a strong forereach and a powerful rear drive.

Rottweilers have an inherent desire to protect home and family.

Front and rear legs are thrown neither in nor out, as the imprint of hind feet should touch that of forefeet. In a trot the forequarters and hindquarters are mutually coordinated while the back remains level, firm and relatively motionless. As speed increases the legs will converge under body towards a center line.

Temperament—The Rottweiler is basically a calm, confident and courageous dog with a self-assured aloofness that does not lend itself to immediate and indiscriminate friendships. A Rottweiler is self-confident and responds quietly and with a wait-and-see attitude to influences in his environment. He has an inherent desire to protect home and family, and is an intelligent dog of extreme hardness and adaptability with a strong willingness to work, making him especially suited as a companion, guardian and general all-purpose dog.

The behavior of the Rottweiler in the show ring should be controlled, willing and adaptable, trained to submit to examination of mouth, testicles, etc. An aloof or reserved dog should not be penalized, as this reflects the accepted character of the breed. An aggressive or belligerent attitude towards other dogs should not be faulted.

A judge shall excuse from the ring any shy Rottweiller. A dog shall be judged fundamentally shy if, refusing to stand for examination, it shrinks away from the judge.

A dog that in the opinion of the judge menaces or threatens him/her, or exhibits any sign that it may not be safely approached or examined by the judge in the normal manner, shall be excused from the ring. A dog that in the opinion of the judge attacks any person in the ring shall be disqualified.

Faults—The foregoing is a description of the ideal Rottweiler. Any structural fault that detracts from the above described working dog must be penalized to the extent of the deviation.

The Rottweiler's temperament is calm and confident.

Disqualifications—*Entropion, ectropion. Overshot, undershot (when incisors do not touch or mesh); wry mouth; two or more missing teeth. Unilateral cryptorchid or cryptorchid males. Long coat. Any base color other than black; absence of all markings. A dog that in the opinion of the judge attacks any person in the ring.*

BIS, BISS, Ch. Rodsden's Tristan v Forstwald, CD, TD owned by Dr. Yvonne Fine.

The Rottweiler Today

When evaluating a Rottweiler what should be remembered first of all is that the Rottweiler is a working breed. His external appearance, basic character, and soundness all reflect

Some early Rottweiler PR on The TODAY Show *with Barbara Walters and Hugh Downs (Feb. 1965). This is Ch. Condor v d Lowenau with Sue Rademacher promoting The Westminster Kennel Club show.*

A/C Ch. Rodsden's Elko Kastanienbaum, CDX, Can. CD, TD, MRC Hall of Fame, ARC Gold Producer participating in the AKC CDX exercise retrieving over the 36-inch high jump.

weighing from 90 to 115 pounds with a height of about 24 to 27 inches, females being proportionally smaller), the Rottweiler is actually the largest of the German utility breeds. A Rottweiler has amazing agility considering his size. One understands how the sleek Doberman can sail over a meter jump; one finds it remarkable that a Rottweiler can do so as well.

Although the original German stud book listed Rottweilers of various colors, the ADRK determined from the beginning to breed only those representatives that were black with tan

that function. A medium large dog (average males

(or the now preferred rust) markings. This color pattern is one of the most noticeable features demonstrating the link with the Rottweiler's offshoot, the Doberman Pinscher. In recent times red Rottweilers have been reported although, as stated in the standard, all base colors other than black are presumed to be from crossbreeding.

The Rottweiler has a short, hard coat with an undercoat varying

"Standard of the Breed" Dog World *1992, Select Ch. Boss v d Biestse Hoeve, CD, TD, BH, SchH III, IPO III, CGC. Owned, trained and handled by Ken Hemmerich.*

in development depending upon the climate. Rottweilers are found from Alaska to Florida although, as a breed developed in northern Europe, they prefer a cool climate. One often sees a Rottweiler happily lying out in the snow for hours at a time. The double coat is also great insulation against water and, if given the opportunity, most Rottweilers will spend as much time as possible in the water. They are great swimmers, aided by their webbed feet.

The Rottweiler is a breed with almost equal proportion of height and length, being ideally nine to ten. Like so many "square" breeds, the Rottweiler has a docked tail (usually

The Rottweiler is a breed with almost equal proportion of height and length, being ideally nine to ten. MRC Specialty Best of Breed A/C Ch. Alck v d Spechte, owned by Sue Rademacher and Elizabeth Eken.

docked at the first joint). Docking may have begun as a response to function—a tail got in the way of a cart or a tail could have been easily kicked by a cow and broken. Most certainly it was a consideration in the overall look of the dog, as the Rottweiler with a long tail appears to be out of balance. Because there has never been any breed selection for tail type, tails left on Rottweilers have no consistency in length, thickness, or carriage. Should docking tails be forbidden, there would certainly have to be modifications made in the present

Rottweiler standard.

The Rottweiler's character saved the breed at the beginning of the century but is causing the breed problems at the end. Rottweilers are extremely intelligent, easily trained, basically even-tempered, and fiercely loyal.

Foremost, they are a guard dog with a great attachment to their master and family and with a corresponding willingness to defend their home. Those temperament traits suited to a protector include self-confidence, the ability to forget unpleasant experiences, and

Although the breed has its dissenters, well-trained Rottweilers make loving family pets.

courage. While these traits in a well-bred and well socialized Rottweiler make for an excellent companion, they can also lead to serious repercussions if not channeled in the right direction. The Rottweiler is simply too smart, too strong, and too self-assured not to be disciplined and trained from the beginning.

Using his carting instinct, this Rottweiler is helping bring in the Christmas tree.

The Rottweiler's basic instincts, including intelligence, trainability, and versatility, have found all sorts of expression for today's fancier. It is still a breed that earns more working titles than championships and leads all working breeds in the number that earn AKC tracking titles.

Rottweilers are good draft dogs and, although that profession no longer exists in the dog world, the ability can still be seen in carting demonstrations, pulling carts and wagons in parades, and weight pulling contests. Most Rottweilers live in suburban or urban settings and yet in the last few years a renewed curiosity in the breed's herding instincts has found an outlet in herding certifications and herding tests sponsored by the Herding Breeds Association. The Rottweiler "pass" rate was so high that it not only impressed the herding judges officiating, but also the AKC. As of June 1,

Six-dog "Budweiler" hitch at the Medallion Rottweiler Club Rodeo.

The Rottweiler's herding instinct remains strong. A herding test is an exciting learning experience for you and your Rottweiler.

1994, the Rottweiler was approved for entry into sanctioned AKC herding events leading to eligibility for still more AKC titles. What is clear from these herding certifications is that the instinct to herd is strong in the breed in spite of dormancy for generations.

Perhaps the most appealing aspect of the breed is that their owners can succeed in so many different endeavors with this utility breed. While devout Rottweiler owners and breeders swear to their beauty, in fact, the Rottweiler is definitely not a glamorous breed. It is a breed which requires very little grooming and pretty much adapts to whatever conditions it faces daily.

Having read this introduction and the breed standard, you realize that the Rottweiler is not for everyone. Remember when considering a Rottweiler that, due to its size and function, it is

A dog run with an insulated dog house provides puppies and older dogs with a great place for exercise and protection from the elements.

obviously not an "apartment" dog unless you are willing to make extraordinary adjustments to compensate for the lack of room. On the other hand, you don't need an estate. A normal-sized, fenced-in yard or a fenced dog run of appropriate size will do nicely. A growing puppy, especially, needs a place of his own where he is not underfoot and where he is not constantly being told "no." And you need a place where the puppy can be secured safely when you have "non-doggy" company. If, however, you decide a Rottweiler will fit with your lifestyle, the

If you decide that a Rottweiler is the breed for you, the next step is to locate a puppy.

next step is to locate a reputable breeder. Most likely you will have to get on the breeder's waiting list for a puppy. Impulse buying or buying a Rottweiler as a gift should not be considered.

When choosing a puppy, consider the whole commitment.
Rottweiler pups need lots of love and attention.

The Rottweiler Breeder

HOW DO YOU CHOOSE A BREEDER?

Even if it is a puppy that you want primarily as a pet, companion, and protector for your family, and you have little interest in showing or breeding, you should look for the very best bred

A good breeder will spend hours playing with and studying his litter in order to get to know each and every pup.

litter you can find, one raised by experienced and dedicated hobby breeders. You have already learned from the introduction and from the AKC standard for Rottweilers that

At five weeks the puppies should still be with their mother.

this is a strong, hard-working breed. You must also learn to read a pedigree. The pedigree documents the puppy's background in depth, listing any achievements of each member of the family tree, such as beauty and working titles. You should also inquire as to whether the parents of the puppy are successfully living in a family situation normal to the United States.

An AKC championship or championship points indicates that somebody besides the owner feels the dog falls within the standard of the breed in beauty and has

Young puppies should be held in your arms on their backs in the submissive position as long as they are little enough to be held as demonstrated by Dutch breeder Tony Huyskens, vh Brabantpark Kennels.

none of the disqualifying faults listed in the breed standard.

American Kennel Club titles are those given in the U.S. at shows sanctioned by the AKC. You may also find in a Rottweiler's pedigree foreign titles, such as Canadian championships and working titles, Mexican championships and working titles, and European titles awarded by the FCI. Some of the European titles are Bundessieger, Klubsieger, Worldsieger, Europasieger, as well as working titles. Generally, beauty titles precede the dog's name and working titles follow the name.

The AKC working titles you might look for in a pedigree are: CD (Companion Dog), CDX (Companion Dog Excellent), UD (Utility Dog), UDX (Utility Dog Excellent), TD (Tracking Dog), and TDX (Tracking Dog Excellent). The AKC has a title that can be earned called the Canine Good Citizen award (CGC). Under

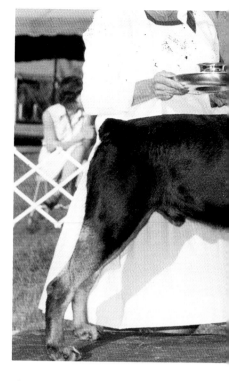

the FCI in Europe, you would have Schutzhund I, II, III, which encompasses tracking, obedience, and protection (sleeve work), ranging from easier to harder

Best in Show Ch. Rodsden's Bruin v Hungerbuhl, CDX shown winning one of many Groups. Bruin was the top-winning Rottweiler of his time. Owned and bred by Jeff Kittner.

FCI is an advanced tracking title, called the FH. BH is a title for the "traffic-sure dog" (a test which evaluates the dog's reactions to such things as traffic situations, strangers, other dogs, etc.) and must be earned before the dog can participate in Schutzhund competition. The whole world has come to realize that it is important for the working dog to demonstrate control when subjected to everyday distractions before he can be taken further into the fun part of his formal training.

What makes the Rottweiler a great working, utility, and family dog are the

exercises. The only separate tracking degree awarded by the

character traits which are bred into him according to the function for which he was intended. From the introduction and the breed standard you have learned what those traits are. You are looking for a stable, dependable, self-confident temperament with a desire to please and a trainability for all things. Working titles are one way of documenting these traits in the pedigree.

A hobby breeder will understand the importance of this documentation and should have demonstrated his understanding by personally having put

A great brood bitch is a joy to any breeder. This is Dagmar v d Biestse Hoeve and her six-week-old pups at Rodsden's Rottweilers.

A breeder will wean his pups onto a good puppy chow by grinding it up and mixing it with warm water. A lamb meal and rice formula is highly recommended.

some of these titles on his Rottweiler. Although titles cannot guarantee perfection, they do tell something about the character of the dog and of the owner. The dog has shown some control under distractions and can be gone over by a stranger, the judge or trainer, without posing a threat. He will stand-stay, sit-stay, down-stay on command and will come when he is called, all things

Good breeders care about where each and every one of their pups are placed.

that could save his life sometime and will certainly save your disposition when living with the dog. Obedience is NOT an option with a Rottweiler; it is a MUST!

We always wonder about breeders who, with no experience in either showing or training, state confidently that they can pick a puppy for you with potential in both areas. Beware of the "instant expert." After all, there is only so much you can learn from books and videos. Unfortunately, when a breed has become too popular its conformation suffers at the hands of the uninformed breeders who only breed for the immediate monetary rewards. There is no shortcut to good breeding!

Rottweiler pups with the credentials to be bred in the first place are, and should be, relatively expensive although you can possibly buy one of the pet-priced pups from a good breeder for less. No matter what you spend on your pup, you want

If you are looking for a Rottweiler to show, a reputable breeder is the best place to go. Four-week-old Rodsden's O. Henry of Cadan is already practicing his stack.

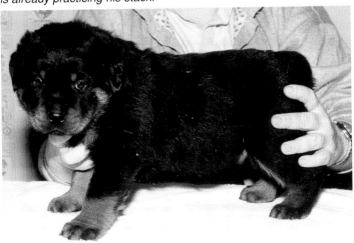

Most importantly, Rottweiler puppies should look like tiny Rottweilers.

often than I would like. (You can imagine how popular a judge it makes me.) On the other hand, although I know that the obligation of the judge is to judge the dog on *that* day in *that* ring without any other consideration, I really hate it when I have completed judging and can look at the catalog only to find that the very good dog I put up comes from a sire and dam with no credentials. Let's face it—that is good luck, not good breeding. The whole theory of purebred dogs is that "like, more often than not, produces like." Otherwise you should go to the pound and take pot luck.

him to grow up to look like a Rottweiler. Too many don't, you know. As a judge, I have had to withhold ribbons for lack of merit or disqualify under the breed standard more

Puppies from a reputable breeder have the advantage of proper early socialization. Tony Huyskens with one of her "Y" puppies.

A good hobby breeder will belong to a breed club, a club formed expressly to educate, provide opportunities to participate in all the AKC and non-AKC canine events, and to offer learning experiences in the breed. In the U.S. we have such clubs that have made it mandatory for their members to at least have a bottom-line, a code of ethics (COE) which defines breeding practices, promotes sportsman-like behavior, and is generally concerned with the welfare of the

Breeders hope for a litter that is so uniform you couldn't tell them apart if their collars were removed.

dog. The three oldest COE clubs in the United States are the Medallion Rottweiler Club (MRC) serving the midwest, the Colonial Rottweiler Club (CRC) on the East coast, and the Golden State Rottweiler Club (GSRC) situated around Los Angeles.

Another thing you should look for on the pedigree and discuss with your prospective breeder is the Orthopedic Foundation for Animals (OFA) certification number for Rottweilers which have been found to be free of hip dysplasia. No dog that has hip dysplasia should be used for breeding. All of the COE clubs in the United States require their members to have their breeding stock radiographed for hip dysplasia and the x-rays submitted to the OFA for evaluation. The OFA issues RO numbers for two-year-old (or older) HD-free dogs and those numbers should appear in the pedigree of any puppy you are considering to buy. To date, the OFA has

Life for your puppy begins with a mother who loves her pups and takes care of them. This loving mother is cleaning her young pup's bottom.

certified over 40,000 Rottweilers.

If you are not working with a COE club breeder, you should ask to see the original (or photographic copy) of the OFA certificates for the sire and dam of the litter. If you are working with COE club members, the litter's pedigree could go back several generations with OFA or have foreign certifications that the dogs were HD free. This does not guarantee that your dog will be HD free, but it does warp the odds in his favor. Again, it is mandatory for the dogs to be OFA certified before being used for breeding in the COE clubs. It is unconscionable for any Rottweilers to be used without this certification. Of course, this does not mean that all OFA certified Rottweilers have the other breed qualifications and should be bred. It does mean that all Rottweilers used for breeding should have an RO number. Do not accept anything less.

WHERE DO YOU FIND A DEDICATED BREEDER?

One of the best ways to find a breeder is to go to a dog show and buy a catalog. Talk to the people at ringside. Then contact those people you find in a catalog and inquire about visiting their dogs at home. A

Good breeding begins with good Rottweilers. Here's Boss owned by Ken Hemmerich.

conformation show introduces the dogs to you under somewhat staged conditions. There might be some ads in the catalog that you can follow up on too. If you've missed the local show, call the local kennel club and ask for help in locating breeders. If you live near a fairground, watch their sign for coming events—"Dog Show Today, Flea Market Tomorrow!"

Go to an obedience school and watch and make inquiries or go to an obedience trial. Both of these are usually

Ch. Falco v h Brabantpark with his sons Ch. Rodsden's Ander v Brabant and Ch. Rodsden's Axel v Brabant.

At bench shows, the dogs that are competing are kept on benches when they are not in the ring. These type of shows are ideal for talking to good breeders.

advertised in the local newspapers.

If you don't live in New York City and don't mind making a long distance call, call the AKC. Their telephone number is listed but, to save you time, call *900-407-7877* which is the AKC's Breed Referral Program. Persons telephoning this number will be referred to representatives of national breed clubs who in turn can give you a breeder to contact in your own

For information and litter listings on Rottweilers visit a breed club booth at a major dog show. This is the Medallion Rottweiler Club's booth at an International Kennel Club show.

geographic area. The national breed club for the Rottweiler is the American Rottweiler Club.

Breeders have to purchase dog food and supplies, so local pet stores or feed stores may also have a few suggestions.

There are a number of dog magazines with pages of Rottweiler ads. Remember, the magazines exist primarily to make money so anyone can advertise as long as he is advertising purebred dogs and has the money to pay for the ad. Be selective. You can sense from the ad which advertisers have genuine interest, rather than commercial interest, in the breed. Many advertisers will list the club or clubs to which they belong. These breed clubs may often have an ad with addresses and phone numbers so you can contact them directly. They, in turn, will have breeder lists and litter listings. Buy a book or video on the breed, either of which should have the author or producer's address in it or

The Medallion Rottweiler Club is a valuable source for both owners and potential owners of Rottweilers.

mention people prominent in the breed.

The MRC runs an ad in the Chicago Tribune on weekends giving phone numbers to call before buying a Rottweiler. Sometimes other clubs in large metropolitan areas also provide this service. Generally, in large metropolitan areas, you should be very careful about answering newspaper ads from individuals. Be especially wary of ads that say, "close out sale," "no offer refused," "will trade for." And "big heads, 160 lbs." raises a flag

Breeders introduce into the whelping box what will become one of the puppies' favorite toys.

every time, as it usually indicates there is little to promote the dogs other than size, which is usually inaccurate. Rottweilers should never be sold by the pound! We also point out that "both parents on premises" is not necessarily a required recommendation. We do suggest visiting the Rottweilers at home, but the stud dog may not be there. The good knowledgeable hobby breeder will have bred his great brood bitch to the dog he thinks is the best male in the country for her and her pedigree. You might not be able to see the stud dog unless you travel.

It is a good idea to visit the puppy at home. You should only buy a puppy sight unseen if you have supreme confidence in the breeder.

Puppies learn the rules of canine behavior from their dam so it is important that although they are weaned, they have playtime with her until they go to their new homes at seven to eight weeks of age.

With breed registration over 100,000 a year, there are thousands of puppies out there and some breeders will tell you anything to get you to buy a puppy. The more knowledgeable you are and the more knowledgeable you sound, the more respect your inquiry will receive and the better puppy you will get.

Remember, you should be working with the responsible hobby breeder who has genuine love and continuing interest in the breed. The breeder has socialized and watched these puppies from birth. You must trust your breeder. As a breeder, I know that the hardest thing about success is getting the right pup to the right people. A successful breeder will have part of the litter reserved in advance. Those on the list who are interested in getting more involved possibly in conformation showing and/or a

Remember that the puppy you choose is yours for life. Approach this decision with equal amounts of logic and emotion.

breed program will also rely on their breeder to select the more promising puppy for them. These pups will be the more expensive ones but they will be from the same litter with the same genetic potential as the less expensive puppy the breeder might select for you.

Successful and respected breeders don't breed "pets." They only mate those dogs who have no disqualifying faults, have good temperaments, are sound, and have won, or could win, on a given day in a conformation show. But large dogs usually have large litters (small dogs, small litters) and so they do not offer them all for the higher prices and with the regular AKC registration.

There is also an optional registration in the AKC called the "limited registration." The pet pups should go out under the limited registration, which means that no offspring from them will be eligible for AKC registration nor are they eligible for AKC conformation shows. They can, however, compete for any of the AKC obedience and tracking titles. Your sales contract, which is also required from COE club members, will spell out which registration you will get. The limited registration has an added advantage in that it can be rescinded by the breeder if the puppy grows out of whatever made him a pet to begin with. The real breeder used to have to put out the pet pups on a spay or neuter contract. Spaying and neutering cannot be rescinded. What a loss and sadness to have a handsome pet come back to visit who is a great working dog and sound and...spayed. Breeders are not infallible. When you are selecting a puppy at seven to eight

The more knowledgeable you are about your breed, the better puppy you can recognize and acquire. This is Rodsden's Juri Von Eppo owned by Kathy Krzyston.

weeks, it is an educated guess. Just be sure your breeder has the right education!

"Trick or treat!"

Selecting a Rottweiler Puppy

There was a time that when you decided to get a puppy, you just went out to a farm and looked at the litter and the pup that ran up to you and kissed you was the one you took home. It doesn't work that way in purebred dogs. Sorry, but if one of the top-priced promising puppies in the litter runs up to you and kisses you first, you still are not going to be able to take that one for the pet price. Sometimes you might have a selection

When you go to pick out your Rottie puppy, bring the whole family along to help in the decision-making process.

The puppy you choose should be friendly and responsive to human contact.

between puppies in the litter, whether for pet or show. In a really good litter, all the puppies should be uniform; if breeders put colored collars on the pups and then took them off, you couldn't tell the difference between the pups. Of course the breeder can! If a litter has only one "pick puppy," then it is not a great litter and the breeder would not repeat that breeding.

Under no circumstances should you be told that differences in temperament determine which puppy is a pet and which is not. All the puppies in a litter should be outgoing, friendly, and responsive to human contact. Sometimes the enthusiasm and energy in which the traits are expressed vary from puppy to puppy, but not their general attitudes.

What a real breeder

This smart little pup has found something to satisfy his chewing needs.

differences. This is the best insurance that you will get that special pup, whether you are buying it as a pet or have a more serious intent.

Discuss with the breeder the various pups in the litter. Find out the differences he sees in the pups regarding conformation and personality. There are some basic things a breeder looks for in the pups which can be seen with some certainty after the pups are six to seven weeks old. The puppy teeth are in by then and you can check the bites. The puppies should have a scissors bite as required by the standard. If the puppy

Although it may seem tempting, giving a puppy as a gift is not recommended.

is striving for is a very good overall litter, uniform, and with only very minor

is overshot, the upper incisors (front teeth) will extend over the lower front teeth so there is a space between them. That pup automatically becomes a pet. The upper teeth should fit tightly over the lower teeth as a scissor. Undershot is just the opposite, with the lower teeth extending over the upper teeth. In 40 years, we have never personally seen an eight-week-old puppy who was undershot, however. The bites can change when the permanent teeth come in and correct or become

Puppies going through the teething period often find things to chew on. The permanent teeth usually don't come in until around four months of age.

incorrect, fortunately or unfortunately as the case may be. The permanent teeth begin to emerge around four months and may show some changes, sometimes up until a year.

Many predominately black dogs might have a white spot or streak on the chest, sometimes extending between the legs. In a Rottweiler this is a serious fault (unless it is just a few white hairs) and such a pup would automatically become a pet. If the spot is very small, it can disappear and you might have the handsomest puppy in the litter later on. This puppy would go to its new home with the limited registration, as would the pup with an incorrect bite. The saving grace is that if either or both corrected, the limited registration could be rescinded by the breeder should your interest in purebred dogs broaden and you wish to get more involved.

Sometimes there is a very small puppy in the litter who will grow up to its genetic potential. Surprisingly, Rottweiler puppies at birth are quite small in relationship to their final size. Well, not as small as newborn Pandas, but actually not much bigger than newborn Dachshunds. Averaging from about

12 ounces to a little over a pound at birth, a small puppy weighing 6 to 8 ounces can mature to Rottweiler puppy to have dark eyes and correct markings. Seven to eight week-old puppies will not

An eight-week-old puppy may not yet have the rich mahogany markings, but the color will start to deepen.

a normal-sized adult, competing successfully in the show ring as well as working in obedience.

You would like your yet have grown the rich mahogany you hope for but the color may well be starting to deepen in the muzzle. The puppies will have a soft, somewhat fuzzy puppy coat but this will change, too. If the pup has long hair on and about the ears, rear, and stomach (and the coat seems to "flow" as the puppy trots around), this may be a long-coated puppy. Long coats are not common but do appear. A puppy with a long coat is, of course, a pet since a long coat is a breed disqualification. There are many other things an experienced breeder looks for that can be pointed out,

Long coats on Rottweilers are not common but they do appear. If the pup you are considering has long hair on the ears, rear and stomach, he may be long-coated. Long coats are a breed disqualification.

A pup should be curious about everything.

which is another reason for coming to a breeder whom you trust.

Puppies should not be allowed a lot of visitors before they have had their first puppy shots at six weeks, which includes the parvo shot. We have not beaten parvo and precautions are key as the virus can be brought in on shoes or clothes. We always remove our shoes before we go into the puppy pen or the room where the puppies are, and we have slip-on sneakers just reserved for wearing in with the puppies.

No matter how concerned you are about parvo, puppies cannot be raised in a "bubble." The family must become the socializers until the pups get to their new homes. Proper socialization and handling from the time of whelping will have been provided by your breeder and are terribly important to the future of your puppy.

You may well be seeing the puppies for the first time when you go to pick yours up so you must realize that one observation is not equal to the breeder's seven to eight-week guardianship. The high-energy little devil in the litter might well have just finished tiring himself out and be sleeping and the quieter, more easygoing one have just awakened! Some breeders do character testing but any test is only as good as the tester. We have never found any significant differences in the puppies when we have done puppy character testing that carried over in adulthood to any degree—the puppy that ran out and brought the crumpled paper ball back has his SchH III degree and the one that ran off with it has his Utility degree. The breeder's selection is still your best bet.

This is Rodsden's Juno of Quira at five months of age.

The ideal time to bring your new puppy home is around seven to eight weeks.

Bringing Home Your Rottweiler

Now that you've settled on a breeder whom you trust and with whom you feel comfortable (and someone who will be available to answer those questions that periodically come up connected with raising a Rottweiler), it's just a matter of being patient until your puppy is ready to go home. According to most animal behaviorists, the ideal time to get your puppy is when the puppy is between seven and eight weeks of age.

Breeders will tell you that by that age puppies long for human companionship. They are much more interested in human interaction than playing with each other and this is the time that the puppy should begin to bond with his new owner. There is no breed where it is more important to establish an early "pecking order" than with the Rottweiler. The puppy must learn from the beginning that you are master and that all your family members precede the puppy.

Of course one can get a puppy at an older age which fits right into the family and older dogs usually adapt very well to a new family—even to a new language, which imports must do. But if you want to have the greatest influence on your puppy's character, the best time to begin is at seven to eight weeks. Also by seven weeks, the puppy will have been weaned for about two to three weeks and will be adjusted to a good commercial puppy chow.

"O Holy Night   Christmas puppy photographed by the author won best puppy photo in the Colonial Rottweiler Club photo contest.

WHAT SHOULD YOU EXPECT FROM THE BREEDER WHEN THE "BIG DAY" ARRIVES?

When you pick up the puppy, he should be accompanied by AKC papers. "Papers" usually take the form of an AKC "blue slip," aptly named because it is blue in color. The blue slip is a form provided by the AKC for each puppy after the entire litter has been registered with the AKC. The blue slip lists the litter's registration number, the name chosen for the puppy, and the transferal of ownership from the breeder to the new owner. All American-bred puppies follow this route of registration—from a litter application to a blue slip to a final individual AKC registration certificate. The blue slip allows the breeder to register the puppy directly to

When you pick your puppy up from a breeder he should be accompanied by registration papers—not newspapers!

Have plenty of toys for your new family member to enjoy once he arrives at his new home.

the breeder, transfer ownership from the breeder to a second party, or specify a limited registration from a breeder to a second party. The limited registration does, as the name implies, limit what can be done with your puppy in AKC circles. With a limited registration your dog can be shown in AKC obedience trials and tracking tests, but not in conformation shows. And again, most importantly, any offspring from a dog with a limited registration cannot be AKC registered. The AKC registration certificates are color coded, a regular registration certificate has a purple border, and a limited registration certificate has an orange border.

With the papers comes the need to decide on a name for the puppy. Everyone who decides on a name for his Rottweiler puppy should remember that the word "noble" is often used to describe the breed. The AKC limits the name to 28 characters and most often the breeder will require that the breeder's kennel name be part of the puppy's registered name. Your breeder may have his kennel name registered with the AKC. Registering a kennel name protects the breeder

The airlines will allow you to take an eight-week-old puppy on board the cabin. Othello is on his way to his new home.

This puppy is familiarizing himself with his new surroundings. Always supervise your pup when he is outdoors.

from the unauthorized use of his kennel name with the AKC (much the same way registered trademarks protect product names). Registering a kennel name requires breeding documentation over a long period of time and a fee paid to the AKC.

Of course you can call your puppy anything, but we've found that using the registered name as the call name, or vice-versa, saves a great deal of confusion later on. For the next ten years, you won't

Remember the name you choose for your puppy stays with him for life. This little puppy's name is Othello.

be explaining why "Max" is really Ch. Hall of Fame's O. Henry. If you hope for a distinguished career for your puppy, chose a distinguished name. Cute names are fine for many breeds and often quite memorable, but the Rottweiler isn't a "cute" breed and what is finally chosen for your puppy stays with him for life. For this reason some breeders prefer to register every puppy to themselves first and then transfer ownership to the new owner, thus assuring

This puppy is familiarizing himself with his new surroundings. Always supervise your pup when he is outdoors.

from the unauthorized use of his kennel name with the AKC (much the same way registered trademarks protect product names). Registering a kennel name requires breeding documentation over a long period of time and a fee paid to the AKC.

Of course you can call your puppy anything, but we've found that using the registered name as the call name, or vice-versa, saves a great deal of confusion later on. For the next ten years, you won't

Remember the name you choose for your puppy stays with him for life. This little puppy's name is Othello.

be explaining why "Max" is really Ch. Hall of Fame's O. Henry. If you hope for a distinguished career for your puppy, chose a distinguished name. Cute names are fine for many breeds and often quite memorable, but the Rottweiler isn't a "cute" breed and what is finally chosen for your puppy stays with him for life. For this reason some breeders prefer to register every puppy to themselves first and then transfer ownership to the new owner, thus assuring that the puppies are named as the breeder wishes. Many new owners add their own name to that of the breeder's name. This is fine if you plan to keep the dog all of his life. The next owner might not appreciate your personalized choice.

The German breeders, as well as many American breeders, name their

Crate training is a great way to housebreak your puppy; but maybe not your child! (It makes a cute photo though.)

litters alphabetically. These breeders require that all the puppies in the same litter have names which begin with the same letter. It may be your luck to choose a puppy from, say, the "Q" or "X" litter! With the puppy should also come health records. By seven weeks, the puppy should have had its first set of puppy shots and have been wormed if a check of stool samples indicates the necessity. The records should be complete and easy for the new owner to understand. The name of the breeder's vet should be included on the records for future

reference by the new owner's vet. An important thing to remember is that the Rottweiler breed is very susceptible to

The crate you choose for your puppy should be big enough for an adult Rottweiler to use at home and to take to dog shows.

parvovirus.

Once the puppy has his own individual registration number, the new owner can request a certified pedigree from the AKC. However, breeders should always provide each puppy owner with their own three or four generation pedigree which may be much more detailed than the AKC pedigree. So many Rottweilers are only a generation or so away from European dogs and AKC pedigrees do not include foreign titles. Also, until just recently, the AKC did not include information on hip dysplasia status. As the widespread xraying of Rottweilers began some 30 years ago, it is quite possible that the pedigree can include generations of dogs whose hip status is known. The pedigree provided by the breeder should be as complete as possible.

Feeding instructions and basic tips are a welcome addition to your puppy's "going-home packet" because they offer help in getting through those first days at home. Helpful information on crate

Always have fresh water available for your Rottweiler.

Some people like to feed their puppy on a raised container that can be raised higher as the puppy grows.

training, housebreaking, names of local obedience clubs, etc., offers answers to questions that may present themselves at all hours of the day and night. When in doubt, call your breeder (although perhaps not at all hours of the day and night!). The breeder is just as anxious as you are to have your puppy become a well-mannered and appreciated member of the family.

One common question asked by prospective owners as they take home their puppy is what size dog crate should be purchased for the puppy?" The practical answer is to recommend purchasing a crate large enough to serve your Rottweiler after reaching adulthood. Crate-trained dogs treat their crates rather like "indoor dog houses." It is a place to retreat for a nap or to just get out of the way. It isn't uncommon to see the adult Rottweiler happily sleeping in a crate with the door to the crate wide open and the choices of "softer" places at hand. If you are purchasing an airline crate, then you will need either a 400- or 500-size crate. A wire crate is preferred because, until the puppy comes to accept (and appreciate) his crate as his special place, he will not feel so isolated in a crate from which he can observe what is going on around him.

It's a good idea to ask your breeder for a small bag of puppy chow the puppy is currently used to eating. Breeders commonly do this. Mixing the old with the new (whatever you decide to feed your puppy) makes the transition period

This little devil has found a new chew toy.

easier on the pup's digestion. Usually a breeder will let the prospective owner know in advance what brand of dog food he recommends.

Finally, the breeder should provide a contract which spells out what each party expects of the other and what is expected of the puppy. The better understanding between breeder and owner in the beginning, the less misunderstandings later on.

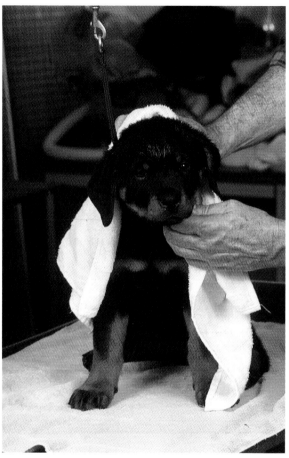

Towel-dry your puppy thoroughly (or you could try "blow drying") after bathing—a wet puppy can become chilled quickly. Owner, George S. Chamberlin.

Grooming Your Rottweiler

The Rottweiler is a "wash and wear" breed. Minimal grooming is required compared to the more fancy breeds with excessive or exotic coats. Rottweilers do, however, shed their coats despite what you may have read to the contrary.

The adult Rottweiler has a double coat—a harsh, straight, and short outer coat as well as a soft undercoat which can be black, gray, or even brown in color. Ideally the undercoat does not show unless the dog is shedding. The undercoat develops as a response to the dog's environment. A dog living in a northern climate, perhaps mostly outside, will have a thick undercoat through the winter while dogs in warmer climates will have very little. The breed standard calls for all Rottweilers to have both coats.

Shedding occurs with both coats but naturally the volume reflects the amount of undercoat present. Rottweiler bitches shed hair after being in season, right before

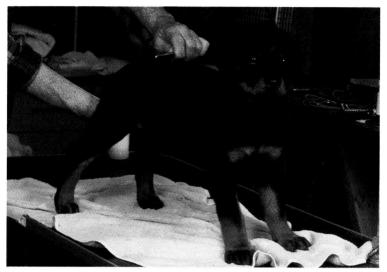

Brushing your puppy daily helps to keep his coat shiny and provides some bonding time for you and your puppy. Owner, George S. Chamberlin.

coming in season, or after whelping a litter. Both sexes may shed in the spring, thus ridding themselves of their winter insulation. Perhaps what has led people to believe Rottweilers don't shed is that the short, black hairs tend to accumulate in dark corners or under rugs while the long, light hairs of the shaggier breeds float in the air for all to see!

A breed disqualification is a long coat. Do not

confuse what is a long coat with a puppy coat. A puppy with a long coat will have a coat that actually "flows" as the puppy trots and a tell-tale sign is long hair on the ears. Long coats are not a common problem but they do occur.

Daily brushing with a stiff brush or a rub with a curry comb serves several purposes. You will be removing any foreign material and dead hairs, you will be stimulating the natural oils which make the coat shiny, and you have another excuse to handle your puppy so that he becomes used to your touch, understands he must submit to being

This well-groomed Rottweiler is a welcomed guest at the wedding of Mr. and Mrs. Duane Mitras.

combed, and learns to stand quietly.

While daily brushing is encouraged, daily baths are not. Bathing a dog often, especially in winter, deprives the coat of its natural oils— not to mention a wet puppy improperly dried off becomes chilled quickly. Washing also tends to make an adult's coat temporarily feel soft which is the opposite of what is prescribed in the standard. For that reason we recommend bathing Rottweilers a few days before taking them to a dog show, rather than the day of the show. Use common sense when you bathe your dog. Keep the soap out of his eyes, use a good commercial shampoo appropriate for a black dog, and be

This is Ch. Rodsden's Ansel v Brabant owned by Ruth O'Brien.

All dogs need to have their nails kept short and most especially "show" dogs! You must learn how to trim your own dogs nails.

sure he is toweled dry.

The breed standard also states that Rottweilers are shown untrimmed. In truth, most professionals at least trim the facial whiskers, although there is a thought that whiskers are another "sense" and greatly missed by the dog if snipped off.

NAILS

What does usually require constant trimming are the toenails, which on Rottweilers are hard, thick, and black making the "quick" hard to locate. A very well-constructed foot means that there is no nail trimming needed. Unfortunately few Rottweilers have perfectly constructed feet—so don't count on the perfect foot when you bring your puppy home. The exceptional dog may enjoy biting back his nails but the "nail biters" never bite back far enough and require a pedicure from time to time. Some Rottweilers don't mind having their feet handled, some really hate it, but all can be taught to tolerate it if you start handling your puppy's feet from the first time he sets them down in your home.

Ask your vet to trim your Rottie's nails every time you visit. This way your pup will become used to being handled and having his nails trimmed, as well as learn to like the vet.

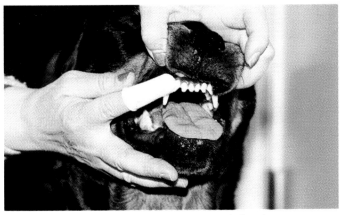

Even dogs need their teeth brushed, especially when you can see tartar build-up. Put the rubber toothbrush on your finger and get to work.

EARS

If your puppy continually shakes his head, it could be a sign of ear problems. Drop-eared breeds are more prone to ear infections so make it a practice to check ears for brown discharge or excessive ear wax. Ears can be cleaned out with cotton swabs and ear cleaning solutions recommended by your vet. Be careful to avoid swabbing too deeply into the ear canal. The good news is that Rottweilers don't mind having their ears cleaned nearly as much as having their nails cut.

TEETH

Tartar tends to build

Playing tug-of-war with Nylafloss is a good way for your dogs to interact and clean their teeth.

up on teeth as the dog matures. You can purchase dog toothpaste and brush his teeth. In more serious cases you can scrape his teeth or have a vet do it. Most owners settle for encouraging the dog to scrape his own teeth by chewing on selected objects such as dog biscuits or nylon or polyurethane bones. We do not recommend giving either puppies or adults real bones to chew on. The strength of a Rottweiler jaw, even in a young puppy, is surprising. Real bones can splinter and when swallowed cause impaction problems.

Also Rottweilers, and probably all other canines, have a different attitude toward real bones and artificial bones. Puppies may tussle over, growl, and snatch each other's toy bones but real bones are guarded with a ferocity, which gives the impression that ownership is a life-and-death matter. The adult reaction is often the same, so don't give real bones of any kind to your Rottweiler. Toy chew-things contribute to healthier gums and stronger teeth, are aids in socialization, and are much safer for all concerned.

Provide your Rottweiler with safe chew toys. The Plaque Attacker™ by Nylabone® has raised "dental tips" to combat plaque and tartar.

You can train your Rottweiler to do almost anything. This Rottweiler is learning how to sit-up.

Training Your Rottweiler

Instruction begins at home, the minute we introduce our pup to his new quarters. In the beginning, it seems as though every other word is "No," just as when we are running after a human toddler. But, eventually, we can attempt various other preschool lessons:

A leash and choke collar are important tools for the initial stages of your puppy's training.

"sit" for a treat, "lie down" while brushing, "stand" for pretty, "stay" for a split second, "outside" for potty, and so on. The dog's vocabulary will increase though yours seems to have regressed. Before you know it, you will need to expand his education and yours.

Most large communities have dog clubs or individuals that offer training classes. People who live in smaller towns or more rural areas may have to search a bit, but can often find trainers within a half-hour's drive. The time spent at classes is well worth the effort.

A good instructor has seen every problem in the book and then some and can give you the benefit of his experience. Someone has always walked in your—and your dog's—footprints, no matter how annoying, embarrassing or frustrating.

Obedience schools usually require that a dog should be six months old or close to it. But there are other alternatives for early socializing and education. Puppy "kindergarten" is fun for everyone, dogs and people alike. Nothing is cuter than a pup, (except a bunch of pups) bouncing, bobbling and *boinnng*ing about. Even the most experienced owner is

Training Your Rottweiler

Instruction begins at home, the minute we introduce our pup to his new quarters. In the beginning, it seems as though every other word is "No," just as when we are running after a human toddler. But, eventually, we can attempt various other preschool lessons:

A leash and choke collar are important tools for the initial stages of your puppy's training.

sit" for a treat, "lie down" while brushing, "stand" for pretty, "stay" for a split second, "outside" for potty, and so on. The dog's vocabulary will increase though yours seems to have regressed. Before you know it, you will need to expand his education and yours.

Most large communities have dog clubs or individuals that offer training classes. People who live in smaller towns or more rural areas may have to search a bit, but can often find trainers within a half-hour's drive. The time spent at classes is well worth the effort.

A good instructor has seen every problem in the book and then some and can give you the benefit of his experience. Someone has always walked in your—and your dog's—footprints, no matter how annoying, embarrassing or frustrating.

Obedience schools usually require that a dog should be six months old or close to it. But there are other alternatives for early socializing and education. Puppy "kindergarten" is fun for everyone, dogs and people alike. Nothing is cuter than a pup, (except a bunch of pups) bouncing, bobbling and *boinnng*ing about. Even the most experienced owner is

set back in finesse, while working with a wiggleworm, trying to avoid stepping on paws and encouraging acceptable puppy manners. Lessons

The Down/Stay exercise. (Above left) *From a sitting position the dog must go down on the verbal command and you are allowed to point to the ground.* (Above right) *The dog goes down and waits for the verbal command to stay. Our thanks to trainer, handler, Sgt. ret. Duane Pickel, K-9 Division Tallahasee Police Department and Yazoo v h Brabantpark, CDX, CGC, TDI, HIC.*

range from sit, stand and stay (for the vet) to nail clipping, basic grooming, walking on leash and coming on command. It's fun and amazing how quickly these youngsters grow, from the tiniest Chihuahua to a mighty Great Dane, and before anyone realizes, it's time to go on to a higher level of education.

Conformation classes often accept puppies as soon as their basic inoculation schedule is in effect, or at about 15 to 20 weeks when they have a titer (immunity) to Parvo. Training for the breed ring consists

The Recall exercise. **Opposite page:**(left) Encourage your dog to come straight to you. (Right)She should sit right in front of you waiting for the command to heel. **This page:** (left)Wait a few seconds and then say the dog's name and "heel." The dog can swing to your side or go around behind you and come to the sit/heel position.(Right) After she sits straight on your left side, praise and pat her for a job well done.

of walking and trotting on leash. The pup learns to stand and allow the "judge" to pet him all over, look in his mouth and examine his testicles. Tips to aspiring handlers are given as well, allowing us to get our feet wet before diving into the big pond of dog shows.

Class training, whether obedience, conformation or kindergarten, teaches the owners how to become and remain the leader in this twosome. Just like a good dance team, one leads and the other follows.

Unless we want a dog who demands us to fetch and cater to his every whim, we'd better learn to lead.

Instructors inform enrollees about the type of leash and collar to use, but most suggest a chain link or "slip" collar, with a

When teaching your dog to heel while on a leash, start with your dog sitting at your left side.

Always step off with your left foot and say the dog's name followed by the heel command.

leather leash. Probably 90 percent of the class simply wants a pet who doesn't jump up on everybody who comes to the door or can walk to the corner without tripping his owner. Class instruction includes basic obedience routines, however, so that the person who wishes to show his dog can do so competitively.

Obedience exercises include heeling (on and off leash), standing, sitting, staying, lying down and coming when called. All of us can take advantage of those handy commands even if we never set foot in a ring.

How nice it is to tell a dog "down" just as he jumps up to greet us with muddy paws or to say "stand, stay" so that the veterinarian can examine him.

Training your puppy to come.
This page: (above) *Put a choke collar and leash on your pup. When he is not paying attention, call his name accompanied by a short, light jerk with the leash.* (Right) *As the pup comes step back and encourage him.*
Opposite page: (above left and right) *As he comes toward you continue to encourage him by saying, "Good Boy. Come."* (Below left and right) *Bring the puppy into to you with lavish praise and encouragement.*

BIS, Select Ch. Ironwood's Cade, CD CGC owned by George Chamberlin. MRC Hall of Fame, ARC Gold Producer.

Showing Your Rottweiler

STARTING WITH A PUPPY

When we started with Rottweilers, over 40 years ago, it was remarkable to see even one Rottweiler at a dog show and there were no specialty shows for the breed. Twenty years ago it was thrilling to find ten Rottweilers at a regular show or, as we thought then, an amazing 100 Rottweilers at a specialty show. In 1992 the largest Rottweiler specialty show in the United States, in the world for that matter, was the Medallion Rottweiler Club's specialty which drew an entry of 900 Rottweilers!

At almost every show across the country, the largest breed entry is usually Rottweilers. This fact mirrors the rapid rise in popularity of the breed and should alert you to what is obvious—that the Rottweiler ring is very competitive. Once upon a time the novice exhibitor could naively show his puppy in the ring, without any preparation, and possibly win. He might have the only puppy entered—not any more. Exhibiting a dog at a dog show is expensive and time-consuming, and it requires planning and training in order to succeed. Oh yes, and it also requires a puppy with conformation worthy of winning. But remember, there are now a great many puppies with good conformation all vying for first place.

The decision to show your puppy was probably made before the puppy was purchased, since your desire for either a show or pet puppy was conveyed to the breeder first thing. If you intend to show your puppy, the puppy should, at seven or eight weeks of age, have no disqualifying faults. True, there are disqualifying faults which can correct with time, such as over-shot bites, but to start from the beginning with a "problem" that you hope will correct is starting with a handicap. Picking a show-winning puppy is, at best, an educated guess and there are plenty of unforeseen "problems" that can pop up along the way.

With the proper beginnings, a promising young pup can grow up to be a champion.

From the time you bring your promising puppy home, you can begin training him for a show career. There is probably no AKC activity more subjective than judging dogs in the conformation ring.

The judge is using his expert eye in determining which dog comes closest to the ideal—his concept of what the perfect Rottweiler looks like as described by the official breed standard. The AKC

By using bait you should be able to teach your puppy to "free stand."

requests that its judges judge approximately 25 dogs an hour, so the judge must make his determinations quickly. For this reason, if for no other, it is imperative that your puppy be taught to look his best during those precious minutes allotted to him by the judge.

Attend dog shows and watch the Rottweiler judging so that before you begin with your puppy you have a picture in your mind of how the puppy should be stacked (standing) for the judge. The Rottweiler is basically a square breed and his legs should be underneath him, usually side by side. You might look at the German Shepherd to compare an entirely different look—the sloping, over-stretched extension of leg popular with the Shepherd is out of place with the Rottweiler. A good rule of thumb is that if the stance you place your puppy in is

Dog shows go on rain or shine. This is Ch. Gasto v Liebersbacherhof, SchH I, CDX, TD handled by Sue Rademacher.

uncomfortable, it isn't correct.

Next watch the judge as he examines each dog. You'll note that he checks the mouth to count the teeth. Rottweilers (in fact most dogs) have 42 teeth, 20 on the top, 22 on the bottom. The Rottweiler breed is one of the few breeds in the AKC where there is a disqualification for missing teeth—two or more missing teeth is a disqualification; any missing teeth is a serious fault. The Rottweiler should also

Move and set your puppy's rear legs by going under the dog's belly and turning and setting the leg from the stifle joint.

Acclimate your puppy to being handled by strangers by taking him to public places.

have a scissors bite, with a level bite being a serious fault. Overshot or undershot dogs are disqualified. So you can see that one of your first goals in preparing your puppy for the show ring is to get him to submit to having his teeth examined. It wastes time for the judge and can be embarrassing for the handler if a puppy resists having his mouth examined. It also points out that you haven't done your homework in getting ready for the show.

During a standing examination the judge will also check for both testicles on the male and generally go over the body,

Practicing with a young puppy on a table helps to keep him still and reduces the amount of bending for the handler.

although the extent of "handling" your puppy by the judge depends on the individual judge's personal technique. Some judges may check coat texture, and that's about all, while others will take their hands and go all over the puppy. Prepare for the latter when training your puppy.

The breed standard states that Rottweilers are natural trotters. Watch the dogs as they are gaited (trotted) individually. Notice that the handler keeps his dog under control on his left side and that the dog moves at a brisk, but not a racing, pace. The object is not to break the natural trot by letting the dog jump, leap, or gallop along.

Now that you have an understanding of the rudiments of showing your dog in the ring you can begin to work with your puppy. Teaching a puppy to stand quietly is your first step. It is sometimes easier to stack a puppy on a table or any surface with which the puppy is unfamiliar because he tends to "freeze" when unsure of his footing. Talk soothingly to your puppy as you practice. Attitude is

The Rottweiler is basically a square breed, his legs should be underneath him.

very important in the ring because the judge is also judging temperament as described in the standard. You'll learn that some puppies are born showmen and some are not. If you haven't a natural showman, you are going to have to work to convince your puppy that all this is fun. Never scare the puppy and keep sessions very short, because stacking a puppy into a perfectly balanced pose may be unnatural for a young puppy who doesn't

Jingling keys can help to get the puppy's attention when practicing stacking.

have adult coordination.

While on the table, examine the mouth. Don't actually try to count the teeth as puppy teeth are very small. There are fewer puppy teeth than the 42 required adult number. What really counts are the adult teeth, which will begin to come in at about four months of age. Just get the puppy used to opening his mouth.When the adult teeth do come in, it is important to check to see that the baby teeth being replaced have been pushed out. If not, you may have to have those stubborn baby teeth pulled so that the adult teeth can take

This six-week-old puppy grew up to become Ch. Rodsden's Parry v Gunter, A/C CD, TD, CGC, HIC. Owner, Howard Bernier.

their proper positions. Getting in the adult teeth is one of the hurdles you and your puppy must overcome on the way to a champion. In fact you might think of a championship as a hurdles race with the

Before a puppy can be trotting along at your side at a brisk pace, known as gaiting, he must be accustomed to walking on a leash.

title at the finish line.

A phenomenon in some puppies that occurs around teething is a tendency for extra folds to develop in the ear, quite often in just one ear and not the other. This is related to increased demands for calcium during the development of the permanent teeth and the size, shape, and natural carriage of the ear. We have not found that giving calcium supplements prevents the problem nor does it seem to help when the folding begins. What is required is to prevent the folds from becoming permanent during the teething. Some ears will straighten out on their own, but don't count on it. Folding, in its extreme, produces a rose ear (so named because the ear resembles a partly opened rose). Massaging the ears frequently will help and most breeders recommend taping the ears in a correct position. Talk to your breeder if you suspect the problem is starting and get his advice on taping. You must be careful when you tape an ear because ear infections can result. Also, you want to be sure you are taping the ear in the right position and not exacerbating the problem. Folding ears is a problem that your

Ch. Rodsden's Porsche Forstwald, CD trained and handled in obedience and Junior Showmanship by her 12-year-old co-owner, Chandra Klem.

breeder will most likely know more about than your vet. Rottweilers with rose ears have finished their championships, but a rose ear can spoil what might otherwise be a very nice head model.

Along with teaching the puppy to stand comes gaiting the puppy. Remember that just as a child can't be expected to run before he has learned to walk, your puppy must first be accustomed to walking on a leash before he is expected to trot along at your side at a brisk pace. Keep your touch light and voice encouraging. This *is* supposed to be fun for

Preparing your Rottweiler for the show ring begins at puppyhood.

At the age of six months you can enter your Rottweiler into a regular AKC dog show.

the puppy. We should mention that when you begin a gaiting pattern, you should focus on a distant point and move towards it. This hopefully will keep you and your puppy gaiting in a straight line, keep you from running into a post while you are concentrating on watching your puppy, and prevent a major mishap (the handler stepping on, falling over, or just plain scaring his puppy to death).

When finally you are convinced the puppy is comfortable with your touch and the gaiting routine,

introduce a third party. Have a family member or friend "play judge." It is important that the puppy, right from the start, accepts strangers. Our standard says the Rottweiler does not lend itself to indiscriminate friendships and some judges get real personal with each dog they examine. Your Rottweiler doesn't have to particularly like it but he must not show that he doesn't like it!

You may now be ready to take the puppy to conformation classes, which obedience clubs offer, and to matches. Matches are set up to

At matches you can practice all that you have taught your dog at home. Specialty giving clubs and all-breed clubs are required to give matches as well as their licensed championship point shows. This is a Medallion Rottweiler Club B-OB match.

provide a forum for clubs to learn how to run real dog shows, for would-be judges to hone their skills, and for novice handlers and puppies to practice.

Your breeder or your local breed clubs can provide you with dates of area matches. Usually once you enter a match, your name is put on a list and you will get notices in advance of future matches. Contact your local Rottweiler club as well, as it probably holds a match for Rottweilers during the year.

With experience in the ring, and your puppy's six-month birthday behind him, you are ready to enter a regular AKC dog show. If you've discovered that you really don't have a talent for handling, you may want to consider the services of a professional handler. A professional handler makes all, or part, of his or her living handling dogs for their owners. The handler usually charges a fee for handling plus board and a portion of travel expenses. The owner is also expected to pay the entry fees for the shows. A handler's reputation as a professional depends a great deal on how successful the dogs are in his care. You may find it expedient, less costly, and easier on your nerves to go the route of a professional. While we recommend that in obedience training you train your dog yourself, we often refer our puppy owners to a professional handler for conformation showing. This is a decision that you will, no doubt, want to discuss with your breeder. Local handlers also conduct handling classes should you decide that you want to be an owner-handler. In our breed we see many very competent and successful owner-handlers. However, all of them have invested a great deal of time in

Ch. Dunja v d Flugschneise, CD owned and trained by Peter Rademacher, Rodsden's Rottweilers.

perfecting their handling skills.

Remember that judging is subjective and only one puppy can get the first place ribbon at each show—so don't be discouraged if it isn't always your puppy. Follow the advice of your breeder, who also has a vested interest in your puppy's success in the show ring. Good luck and have fun!

International A/C Ch. Barto v t Straotje, IPO III, A/C TD owned by Frank Fiorella.

THE DOG SHOW SPORT

There are shows, and then there are shows.

All-breed shows and trials offer a bit of everything. Each entry is a purebred dog of a recognized breed, and at all-breed shows, there may be as many as 130 or more breeds entered. Trials are for obedience competition and may be held in conjunction with breed shows. Specialty shows are for one breed only, and national specialties are hosted by the national "parent" club, usually accompanied by a great deal of hoopla.

In the US, the Rottweiler is exhibited in the Working Group. In Canada and England, however, there is no Herding Group so the Rottweiler competes against herding breeds, such as the German Shepherd and the Bearded Collie, which are all in the Working Group.

Field trials, tracking tests, hunting tests, herding tests and trials and other instinct tests are usually held outdoors and are often hosted separately. Instinct, agility and temperament tests are offered as added attractions more and more frequently at large all-breed and national shows.

At one time, all shows were benched with entries tied to their cubicles for spectators to observe. Now, benched shows

BISS, BIS Ch. Rodsden's Tristan v Forstwald, CD, TD tracking in the snow with Peter Rademacher.

Medallion Rottweiler Club Hall of Famer Ch. Asta v Forstwald, CD owned by the author.

have declined, and few are still in existence. Every dog lover should attend at least one of these benched events, either as a competitor or spectator. Some exhibitors decorate their benches and spread picnic lunches on grooming tables. Since the dogs are required to stay on their benches for several hours, it's a good opportunity for showing off the breeds, sharing knowledge, making contacts, observing other breeds, talking "dogs" and having a good time. At other exhibitions, it's usually "show and go."

Competitive events are showcases for the breeders' best.

Sometimes it's more fun to observe, but true enthusiasts will tell you that when they aren't competing, they feel the itch.

As with any other

A typical outside show on a beautiful sunny day. This is Ch. Rodsden's Toni v Forstwald, A/C CD owned and handled here by Sue Rademacher.

BISS A/C Ch. Nordike's Aluger v Lindenwood, a top-winning Rottweiler handled here by Mike Conrad and owned by Thomas and Laura Wurstner.

passion, showing is a progressive disease. It starts slowly with a yen to have the dog behave and show well, to be in the placings, to obtain a leg or a point. Once that goal is attained, excitement mounts and the drive is on to reach the top in our field: Championship, a Best of Breed, a Group I, a Best in Show, Top-winning Dog; a High in Trial, a 200 score, an OTCh,

Super Dog at the Gaines Classic; a field or herding trial placement, an instinct Championship, National Gun Dog Champion.

DOG SHOW MANIA

Most first-time buyers have no interest in showing. Oftimes the show bug bites the unsuspecting shortly after joining a training class. Following the initial exposure, the future show addict weakens and the "disease" settles in for a long-term stay and occasionally is terminal.

As the weeks proceed, we note how smart and/or beautiful our dog is compared to the others in the class. When a notice is passed about a nearby match, we decide to enter just for the fun of it. That's why it's called a fun match.

People go and have a good time, and so do the dogs. The atmosphere is relaxed, other novice exhibitors and untrained pups are entered, and although winning makes the day even more fun, competition is not intense. Win or lose, those who have succumbed to the bug soon find another match or two and then begin thinking about shows.

MRC President Joan Klem presenting trophy for High Score in Veterans Obedience and High Score in Obedience handled by a junior to her granddaughter, Chandra Klem and Ch. Gasto v Liebersbacherhof, SchHI, CDX, TD.

Time marches on, and so do we . . . to the beat of a different drummer. Weekends are consumed by showing and doggy interests: conformation, obedience, field trials and instinct tests. Week nights we attend club meetings to plan these events. Our wardrobe consists of tweeds, mohairs, washable suits, all with running shoes to match and with pockets for bait.

The family vehicle has grown from a sedan to a station wagon or van, and it bears a bumper sticker saying, "I'd rather be at a dog show." Realtors start

Rottweiler clearing the high jump at an outside obedience trial.

Rottweiler performing scent discrimination in the Utility Class at an obedience trial.

calling about the five acres for sale just outside of town.

By this point, the enthusiast is eyeing another dog or three and planning the kennel building with indoor/outdoor runs. Often our first dog does not take the pro world by its ear, and we decide that ol' Phydeaux can enjoy life by the fireside while we set forth to search for the Wonder Pup that stirs the judges' blood.

Depending on our experience and knowledge, we demand *top show quality* and qualify this with specifics: showmanship, natural instinct, a gorgeous head,

At a specialty show, a best of breed win is the equivalent of best in show. Here Ch. Rodsden's Tristan v Forstwald, CD, TD is winning the Medallion Rottweiler Club show in June of 1984. Owner, Dr. Yvonne Fine.

superior movement, intelligence, and so on.

We know what we want—perfection. The trick is obtaining or breeding that ideal . . . or even coming close to it. That's what showing is all about: the quest for the ideal. To reach that unreachable star. It's not exactly tilting at windmills, because some come close—close enough to touch the star's tip, to be thrilled by its warmth. But perfection has not yet been attained. No dog scores 200 every time it walks into the obedience ring, and never has one remained unbeaten for its career in the breed ring.

CLUBS

Joining a club is

BIS, BISS Select Ch. Tobants Grant owned by Joseph W. Thompson shown here winning under judge Sue Rademacher.

probably the best way to learn, advance and eventually help others attain their goals. Almost anywhere there are dogs, there is a dog club. More than 3,000 dog clubs exist, and these clubs host approximately 10,000 AKC-sanctioned events annually.

Clubs bring together people interested in a common cause, in this case, their dogs.

Best in show is selected from the winners of all seven groups at an all-breed show. This is BIS, BISS Ch. Nelson v h Brabantpark, a top-winning Rottweiler and MRC Hall of Fame and ARC Gold Producer, owned by Michael Grossman and Clara Hurley.

Most clubs hold annual shows. This is Ch. Vom Sonnenhaus Krugerrand, CD shown winning under the author at an American Rottweiler Club show adding BISS to his title. Went on to become MRC Hall of Famer and ARC Gold Producer.

Whether we want to attain a conformation or obedience title, to breed better animals or simply to enjoy our canine companion, we can do it in the company of others who love dogs.

It's encouraging to have friends cheer us on in our attempts. Tailgate parties are more fun when friends are along, and when several club members attend a show, there's usually someone who has cause to celebrate.

Most clubs hold annual shows, matches and other doggy events, such as instinct tests, seminars, demonstrations and training classes. A list of breeders within the

At Specialty shows a judge may award a certain number of awards other than best in specialty show, best of opposite sex, and best of winners. The American Rottweiler Club calls such awards "Select." The dog's title would then be "Select" Ch. Boss v d Biestse Hoeve, CD, TD, SchH III, IPO III, CGC.

Ch. Susan v d Hoeve Cor Unum, CD owned by Susan Rademacher.

club is made available to those searching for puppies or studs.

Most important, a club consists of members. Members who hold our hand when our pal is in surgery, who bring the bubbly when our dog finishes and who offer advice and company during a whelping.

It's having friends who help us through the hard times or who hold an extra dog at ringside. No matter what happens, someone has already walked in our shoes. When we come in fifth out of five, have a pup going through the teenage ganglies or own a bitch who has trouble conceiving, someone can usually console us and either offer advice or supply the name of someone who can. Being a club member means we can have company who doesn't care about dog hair in the coffee and who comes to visit wearing jeans already marked with paw prints.

Club membership is caravaning to shows, helping to tow another out of a mud-sucking field or jump-starting a battery on a sub-zero day. Members care about each other and about their dogs.

TRAINING

Training classes are offered through these organizations and by experienced individuals. Although it's possible to train a dog without attending a class, it's difficult to test an animal's abilities without distractions. With other dogs and people around, our dog may find them more interesting than our commands. But dogs have to learn to behave under any circumstance. Many an owner claims, "I can't understand it. He's does it all fine at home."

The author and her house dog, MRC Hall of Famer ARC Gold producer Ch. Eppo v d Keizerslanden, CDX, BH, Can. CD at a Canadian dog show.

Obedience training inside on mats is routinely held by many obedience clubs. It is important for your dog to get used to as many different places and situations as possible.

A class instructor knows how to solve a problem when teams are at a stalemate in an exercise and can correct us when we're doing something wrong to lead the dog astray. Besides, group training is sure more fun than doing it by ourselves.

Training is valuable for all dogs and all owners, not just those who are going into competition. Probably 80 percent of all people who register for a training class simply want a well-behaved companion. The all-important bonding is intensified when dog and master learn to work together and develop respect for one another.

Training doesn't stop with class, however. It continues at home, through practicing the stack, the stay, moving on leash, and through bringing out the best in our dogs by conditioning them.

CONFORMATION

Exhibitors who like conformation showing champion the cause with gusto. It's more than just a beauty contest, enthusiasts claim. It's an attempt

Give the command "stay" without using the dog's name (remember this is a stay exercise) and with the palm of your hand in front of the dog's nose. Then leave stepping out with your right foot (stay command, right foot; moving command, left foot).

to breed the dog closest to the standard, improving on each generation. It's being instrumental in the creation of a dog who causes a sensation, a murmur in the crowd, and always draws the spectators and surreptitious glances from the judges in the adjoining rings.

It's handling that dog to countless Best of Breed (BOB), Group and Best in Show (BIS) wins, smashing records and setting new ones. And moving around the yard with a youngster who never sets a foot down wrong and knowing . . . just knowing . . . that this is the one that will take you all the way,

close enough to snag that star.

We soon learn the jargon and doggy etiquette. Fifteen points make a Champion; nine of these points may be obtained in minor (one or two-point) competition. Two majors (three-to-five points) are required, and at least three judges must have found the dog worthy of receiving points.

Majors are do-or-die occasions. Because majors are almost as scarce as tickets to the World Series and just about as difficult to win, one does not cause that major to break by withdrawing a dog unless one has a death wish.

BISS Ch. Rodsden's Kane v Forstwald, CD. MRC Hall of Famer and ARC Gold Producer. Owners, J. Klem and E. Thompson.

Ch Gasto v Liebersbacherhof, SchH I, CDX, TD, handled here by Cindy Meyer. Owned by Rodsden's Rottweilers, reg. MRC Hall of Famer, ARC Gold Producer, trained by Pete Rademacher.

But all of this starts with a first training class, where the handler and the pup learn to walk, and then run, without tripping over each other. Here the trainer teaches the handlers to bring out the best in their dogs and to look graceful while doing so. Some of us never attain this ability and hire a professional to do the job.

Handlers are convenient. Showing is their job, and they don't have bosses grumbling when they take time off work to attend events.

Because they are able to travel and participate in more shows, their dogs win more frequently. Because their dogs win more frequently, they attain more clients and compete more often, and win

Ch. Rodsden's Tristan v Forstwald, CD, TD, BIS, BISS 1984 and 1988 MRC Specialties. Dr. Yvonne Fine, owner.

more often, and on and on and on.

Breeders often have other commitments besides jobs. There are spouses, "What! You're going another weekend?" Children, "But, Dad, I wanna go to the beach." And whelping demands, "So you want me to cross my hocks until you come back, or what?"

Because handling is their career, pros have the experience and finesse amateurs often lack. When a person spends 40 hours a week doing something, he or she is usually more competent than those of us who eke out an

Portrait of Harras. Judged to be the most impressive Rottweiler ever.

Chandra Klem winning Best Handler in Junior Showmanship at MRC Specialty.

hour or two of our spare time.

Occasionally, an owner doesn't attend any of the shows but sends the dog off with a professional until the Championship or honors sought are attained. Once the decision is made to hire a pro, we must decide who is the best for our dog. Most

Ch. Rodsden's Parry v Gunter, A/C CD, TD, HIC, CGC shown winning a "major" on his way to his championship. Owned, trained, handled by Howard Bernier. Winners dog and winners bitch are awarded the championship points and then go on to compete for Best of Winners.

handlers specialize within a group or type. For instance, one person may handle all terriers, but nothing else. Another concentrates on "coaty" dogs, such as the Poodle, Bichon Frise and Pomeranian.

Find out who wins consistently at shows

and ask other owners for advice. Observe, also, the handler's treatment of her dogs. Does she truly like dogs? Do she and her dogs look like a team when competing? Or is this only a way to earn extra money on weekends?

Ask to watch the grooming session. Is he thorough, yet gentle? Do his charges like him? Notice

Ch. Falco v h Brabantpark, Dutch import shown going Best of Winners at MRC Specialty. Owner, handler, Pat Rademacher.

whether he is firm or rough in his methods. Cleanliness of facilities and exercise areas counts too.

Owners should be compatible with their dogs' handlers, and so should the animals. If there is a personality clash, someone's going to lose. Most times, it's the dog.

Ascertain the fees before making any verbal or written agreement to hire someone. A few professionals charge a higher fee per show, but cover expenses themselves. Most charge expenses in addition to their fee.

You may be able to share expenses if the handler has several other clients, but that usually means sharing time as well. Ask what happens when she has a conflict in another ring. Some handlers have assistants or work out reciprocal agreements with other pros.

Discuss all possibilities in advance: veterinary care, bonuses for special wins, splitting of cash awards, length of commitment, and so on. Even if you send your dog with the handler for a period of time, she should call regularly to let you know how he's doing and to work out further details. That's the meaning of—and the reason for—a professional.

Nine-year-old Ch. Rodsden's Quinella of Wylan. Owner, Cindy Mann.

Everyone has different methods of obtaining goals. With some, the game is incomplete unless they themselves breed, train and exhibit their dogs. Others are content with buying a superstar and cheering from the sidelines. Still others fall somewhere in between. Whatever the route, the final destination is the same, to own a dog that excites the senses—and the judge.

For many exhibitors, the challenge lies at specialty shows. Winning under a judge who has a depth of knowledge about—and perhaps has bred, owned and/or exhibited—this particular breed is a coup, particularly when the win is over

Ch. Rodsden's Toni v Forstwald, A/C CD going Best of Opposite Sex, owned by Joan Klem and Sue Rademacher.

a large number of other quality entries. Gaining the nod at a national specialty show is especially gratifying. There will always be a thrill at being chosen the best among one's peers.

Most people compete at all-breed shows frequently, however, possibly because there are more of these events than specialties. Here the excitement mounts as each hurdle is met and overcome: the class win, Winners, Breed,

Ch. Rodsden's Kelso v Forstwald. J.D. and Eleanor Brinkley, owners.

Group and ultimately BIS. These achievements feed the progressive urge to conquer.

OBEDIENCE

Many owners sign up for a training class, hoping the results will give them a well-behaved pet. At discovering the yet untapped intelligence of our dogs, we yearn to find out just how good they really are.

For many owners, the goal is to gain titles (Companion Dog, CD; Companion Dog Excellent, CDX; Utility Dog, UD) which proclaim their pets' ability and their own prowess in training. Three passes (or legs) under three judges, and that's enough.

But a few hone the competitive edge, going for an Obedience Trial Championship (OTCh), as well as top wins in individual breeds and in all-breeds. To win an OTCh, the dog must garner 100 points from winning first or second placings in Open and Utility Classes against all breeds, including those who already have their OTCh. Capturing High in Trial (HIT), whether at an all-breed, specialty or national show, is a coup that all serious competitors seek.

Special trials such as the Windsor Classic, the Gaines Regionals and Classic—which is considered the Super Bowl of the obedience world—attract the

Int., Mex., A/C Ch. Rodsden's Goro v Sofienbusch, A/C Mex. UDTX, Can. TDX, SchH I, clearing the utility bar jump. Owned, trained, and handled by Jim Fowler.

The biggest thrill you will ever have is earning a Tracking degree with your Rottweiler. Rottweilers are terrific trackers and rank high among breeds earning TD and TDX titles in the AKC.

best working teams in the country. Amazing precision does not remove the obvious pleasure of the dog to be working with his best friend.

All of this brings the bonus of a good companion, one with enough manners to keep his nose out of the guests' cocktail glasses and who waits politely for his own potato chip without too much drooling or too many mournful looks.

TRACKING

When it comes to tracking, our dogs always beat us by a nose. Canines have 40 times more olfactory sensory cells than humans do, and that's why they have such busy noses. Why not put to good use all that business of tracing down every crumb on the floor and sniffing at each

You begin to teach your dog to track by showing him the glove and the food "treat" you are laying on it or in it. The "end of the rainbow" comes when he finds the glove at the end of the track.

other and visitors in embarrassing places?

Tracking, unlike the other obedience titles, can be earned at any time, before the CD, after the UD or anywhere in between.

A dog's been using his nose since birth when he followed it to his mother's table setting. Allowing the dog to do what comes naturally is not always easy for owners, however, because we're used to running the show. Training to track often consists of teaching the handler to "lay off" and to take directions from the dog, as well as steering the dog's nose in the right direction and on command.

The second hardest thing about tracking is forgetting about creature comforts. Tracks are laid in the rain, the cold and the heat, as well as on beautiful, balmy days. They're laid in muck and frost and amongst ragweed tickling our noses, as well as in lovely, grassy pastures. Over hill and dale in addition to flat surfaces. You get the picture—training must also be performed under such conditions so that the dog tracks during any trick of Mother Nature. Not only that, early morning is the best time to train while the dew is still on the roses. . . and the ground.

If you and your dog hold up to snuff and enjoy the great outdoors, then there's the TDX (Tracking Dog Excellent).

HERDING AND FIELD TRIALS

Each of these have stylized the trials for the type of dog, i.e., spaniel vs. pointer vs. retriever; shepherd vs. collie vs. cattle dog. In other words, a German Shorthaired Pointer is not expected to do field work like a Golden Retriever or an English Springer Spaniel. A Shetland Sheepdog works a flock differently than a German Shepherd

Working your Rottweiler has many joys, not the least of which is having the "star" in the class. Ch. Iolkos v Dammerwald, CD. Owned, trained and handled by the author.

or a Corgi does.

If you like the combination of dogs and horses and you have a Beagle, Basset Hound, Dachshund or sporting dog, then field trials might be your bag. Locating and pointing hidden game birds are the object of this sport. Dogs (and handlers) must be steady to the sudden flushing of birds to wing and to the noise of guns.

Dogs work two at a time, in a brace, for up to an hour with

To test if the Rottweiler's herding instinct is still in tact, the Herding Association conducts herding tests. As of June 1, 1994 Rottweilers can comppete in AKC sanctioned herding trials.

The Rottweiler does very well in herding tests as the instinct remains strong...and it is another "fun" thing to do with your Rottweiler.

handlers and judges following on horseback. When a point is made, the handler flushes the birds, the official gunners shoot the bird and the dog is sent to retrieve. Wins are judged on verve, style and stamina as well as manners.

Field trials are also held on foot after rabbits for Beagles, Bassets and Dachshunds. Sharp working dogs may attain a Field Trial Championship.

Herding trials follow an obedience format, with three passes to attain a title, three titles and a Championship title: Herding Started (HS), Herding Intermediate (HI), Herding Excellent (HX) and Herding Champion (HCh).

Cattle, sheep, goats or ducks may be used as stock in course A (for driving and farm/ranch dogs such as Australian Cattle Dogs, Bouviers, Corgis, Smooth Collies and Old English Sheepdogs). Sheep or ducks may be used in course B (fetching, gathering type dogs, such as Border Collies, Rough Collies, Beardies and Shelties). Sheep are used in course C for boundary herding dogs such as Pulik, Briards, German Shepherds and the Belgian herders. Each course has specific requirements. A Malinois who works like a Bouvier is not required to enter course C; however, he may be entered in course A.

CANINE CITIZENSHIP

In an effort to promote responsible dog ownership and good canine members of society, the AKC approved the Canine Good Citizen Tests in 1989. We have long since passed the time when dogs were allowed to roam at will—creating destruction, havoc and more puppies or alternatively being fed

Ch. Rodsden's Vikon v Eppo, CDX, TD, BH, TT, SchH III, nationally ranked in obedience. Owner, Angela Schroeder.

Inca, an eight-month-old Rottweiler, playing with a 14-month old boy. Great temperament and great buddies.

by the butcher, the baker and the candlemaker with benign good will. Today's dog must learn to adapt to modern, crowded society.

Dogs perform the tests on leash and are graded either pass or fail. The evaluators consider the following:

1. Does this dog's behavior make him the kind of dog which they would like to own?

2. Would this dog be safe with children?

3. Would this dog be welcome as their neighbor?

4. Does this dog make his owner

AKC approved Canine Good Citizen Tests promote responsible dog ownership and good canine members of society.

happy—without making others unhappy?

There are ten tests. The dog must:

1. Be clean, groomed, healthy, and allow touching and brushing by the evaluator.

2. Accept a stranger's approach.

3. Walk on a loose lead under control—as though out on a walk.

4. Walk through a crowd.

5. Sit for an exam while a stranger pets him.

6. Sit and down on command.

7. Stay in position.

Additionally, the entry is judged on its reaction to:

8. Another dog.

After tracking comes obedience in a Schutzhund trial. Heeling through a crowd is one exercise.

9. Distractions such as loud noises, sudden appearance of a person or a person with an object such as a bicycle.

10. Being left alone for five minutes.

SCHUTZHUND

Some people think Schutzhund is aggression training. On the contrary, an aggressive dog is a detriment. One of the requirements is the ability to call the dog off a hold or "grip."

Schutzhund encompasses various tests, including obedience and tracking, as well as protection. During the protection phase, the dog is expected to search, find, guard and pursue a suspect, who is actually a decoy dressed in padded overalls and a padded sleeve.

The dog is also expected to protect himself and his handler during attacks. All bites must be on the padded sleeve and stopped on command or when the attacker surrenders. The United Schutzhund Clubs of America state, "The protection tests are intended to

Schutzhund protection work...the courage test.

Schutzhund protection work. Search the blinds for the bad guy/decoy, then hold by sitting in front of decoy and barking.

INSTINCT TESTING

During the 1980s, the American Kennel Club encouraged getting back to the basics training with instinct tests. Their hunting tests began in 1985 and have been enormously successful, growing faster than anyone expected.

In 1990, AKC approved herding tests as a sanctioned sport. National clubs encourage natural instincts by sponsoring water tests for Newfs, tunnel tests for terriers, lure coursing for sighthounds, coaching trials for Dalmatians, weight pulling and carting for working dogs, and

assure that the dog is neither a coward nor a criminal menace."

In 1990 the AKC Board of Directors voted to prohibit any AKC-licensed or sanctioned club from sponsoring or advertising Schutzhund or similar activities.

sledding for nordic breeds. The only test for toy breeds at present is a daily one for all dogs—companions for their owners.

All of these instinct tests are pass or fail. Either the dog does it . . . or he doesn't. This format is great for the pet owner who simply wants to see if his dog can do what he was supposed to do 100 or more years ago when the breed was first developed. The tests are also a way for the show exhibitor to prove that, yes, his dog can do more than be pretty. Yes, he can work like he was meant to.

Rottweilers love carting all over the world, even in Australia.

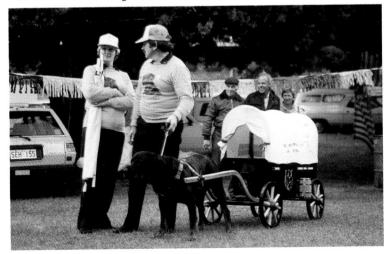

Hunting tests are divided into Junior, Senior and Master stakes with different formats for retrievers, pointing dogs and flushing spaniels. Basic herding test classes are divided Preliminary and Principal. When the dog has passed both, he receives an HT (Herding Tested). The more complicated Pretrial Test shows more advanced training and a passing dog receives a PT (Pretrial Tested).

When a dog has never before been trained or exposed to his erstwhile duties, it's amazing and exciting for owners to watch a dog "turn on." As the dog's attention is caught, his posture changes to one of alertness. Eyes become intense and muscles twitch in readiness.

These tests are also good news for the

Rottweilers are excellent carting dogs. Notice the custom-fit harness on Ter Waele's Erich, CD, TD, BH, CGC, pulling young Master Perrin Gardner Rademacher.

person who is non-competitive or has limited time or budget to spend on doggy activities. Further information on these events may be obtained from the American Kennel Club, Performance Events Dept., 51 Madison Avenue, New York, NY 10010, and through books written on these particular subjects.

Yes, a dog can be attractive and conform to the standard and can still work. Maybe next, truffle hunting trials for Poodles.

AGILITY

Agility is almost more fun than work, and it's certainly fun for those watching it. Although a few people are beginning to take it seriously, most entries simply want to see if their dog can and will conquer the obstacles.

Originating in the United Kingdom in 1977, agility has begun popping up at more and more American shows as well. The object is for the dog to take on each obstacle as quickly as possible and without making a mistake. These include jumps, a scaling wall, a rigid tunnel, a collapsible tunnel, a hoop, seesaw, wall, water jump and almost any

Agility has gained widespread support for all breeds. For a big dog, the Rottweiler does very well. This Rottweiler is going through the tunnel.

The window jump.

other barrier a club can invent. There are also a table and a pause box, where the dog must stand on top for five seconds.

The best time and performance wins. Relay teams increase the challenge and fun. Clubs may offer courses for large dogs and for small dogs. Agility is held as a non-regular obedience class under AKC rules.

THE INGREDIENTS FOR SUCCESS

Showing attracts young and old people of all shapes, sizes

and ethnic origin, with their young and old dogs of all shapes, sizes and breeds. As in all situations, the human personalities vary, but the most successful dogs display confidence, enjoyment of the sport, and that elusive word "presence." Depending on the breed, a spectator might describe a dog as noble, regal, winsome, cute, amazing, smart or delightful. In all events, dogs displaying viciousness are disqualified.

Both owners and dogs should possess and exhibit enthusiasm for their sport, no matter what the arena. If it's not there to begin with, it sure won't be after heartbreaking defeats, treks through blizzards and dropped majors. Sometimes even hundreds of blue ribbons can make you feel blue! Therefore, whatever the sport, the main ingredient is loving dogs and doing things with them.

Schutzhund obedience...the retrieve over the 1 meter high jump.

Adult Rottweilers love to swim and puppies can be taught to love it, too.

Your Rottweiler's Health

You have arrived home with this great puppy and all the breeder information, now what do you do about caring for your puppy at home? Health, socialization, training: which

Proper care includes regular visits to the veterinarian for checkups on heart, ears, and teeth.

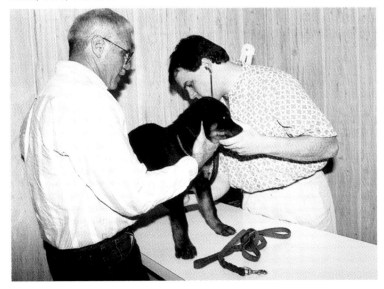

comes first? That is like asking, which comes first, the chicken or the egg? Actually, they all come first or, rather, they all need your attention simultaneously.

Soon after you bring your pup home, it is a good idea to have your veterinarian check him over and review the shots he has already had. Don't forget to take the health certificate and immunization record with you to assist your vet in outlining the regimen that he prefers. Be sure to point out that Rottweilers are more

Health, socialization, and training all occur simultaneously. This Rottweiler is having some fun in the yard with his little sister.

At 8 to 9 months, your pup will sit and stay and down and stay, you hope.

susceptible to parvo than are other breeds so they should receive a parvo vaccine every three weeks until they are 20 weeks old. Pups can have a blood test to show if they have developed a titer (immunity) to parvo. If not, continue the parvo shots until your puppy does show a titer. Corona is a parvo-type infection and needs continuing immunization also. A yearly booster is a good idea, as well as one before you attend obedience class or dog shows. If you have to leave your dog in a boarding kennel, the kennel will probably require that his shots be up to date. Do give your Rottweiler a parvo and corona booster shot, unless he has had one within the previous month or so.

Many canine diseases can now be prevented through vaccinations. We recommend that you follow a schedule prepared by your veterinarian. Listed below are the most important diseases for which vaccines are currently available.

Canine Distemper is a widespread, often fatal disease. All dogs should be vaccinated

Here are a few of my favorite things.

against distemper, starting with a distemper-measles vaccination at six to nine weeks of age.

Canine Adenovirus Type 1 and Type 2 cause infectious hepatitis and respiratory infection, respectively. Hepatitis caused by Adenovirus Type 1 may cause severe kidney damage or death. Adenovirus Type 2 is an important factor in kennel cough.

Canine Leptospirosis is a bacterial infection which may lead to permanent kidney damage. The disease is easily spread to other pets and humans.

Ch. Afra v Hasenacker, SchH I, CD. Owned by Rodsden's Rottweilers.

Canine Parainfluenza is another cause of kennel cough. Although parainfluenza is often a mild respiratory infection in otherwise healthy dogs, it can be severe in puppies or debilitated dogs.

Canine Parvovirus Infection is a disease

"Sofie" at Christmastime. Dr. Ergas, owner.

disease that causes vomiting and diarrhea in dogs of all ages. Dehydration from Coronavirus infection can be life-threatening especially in young puppies.

Rabies one of the world's most publicized and feared diseases, is almost always fatal. The rabies virus attacks the brain and central nervous system and is transmitted to humans chiefly through the bite of an infected animal.

Canine Bordetella (B. Bronchiseptica) may contribute to kennel cough. This bacterial infection can occur alone or in a combination with distemper,

of widespread distribution which may cause severe dehydrating diarrhea in dogs of varying ages. Parvovirus infection is especially dangerous for puppies.

Canine Coronavirus Infection is a highly contagious intestinal

Adenovirus Type 2 infection, Parainfluenza, and other respiratory problems.

Lyme Disease is a complex illness causing arthritis, severe pain, fever and lameness caused by bacterium called Borrelia burgdorferi. It is passed on by ticks and affects wild and domestic animals, including dogs, as well as humans.

The vet who provided the above list uses the following schedule for

A Rottweiler mom looks after someone else's children.

Rottweiler puppies:

1st DM parvo at six weeks with corona, 2nd parvo at 8 weeks with corona.

2nd DHLPPC at ten weeks, 3rd DHLPPC at 12 weeks with Lyme.

4th DHLPPC at 14 weeks, Rabies at 16 weeks with bordetella.

5th and 6th parvo at 17 and 20 weeks (check after two weeks for titer) for parvo. If pup shows no titer, continue parvo until he does.

All this sounds like your puppy will be treated like a pin cushion at every veterinary visit, but actually these immunizations can be combined into one or two shots at each visit.

FLEAS AND PARASITES

There are four common internal parasites that may infect your dog: roundworms, hookworms, whipworms, and tapeworms. Coccidia seems to lie dormant until your pup is put under stress and then it might surface. Always take a stool sample so your vet can check for these parasites and give you the proper medication for your pet. Checking for parasites is a continuing duty to ensure good health throughout your adult dog's life.

A pair of MRC Hall of Famers, A/C Ch Rodsden's Elko Kastanienbaum, CDX Can. CD, TD and Ch Asta v Forstwald, CD. They are two examples of what you look for in the breed: handsome, great workers, great producers, and great companions!

External parasites (fleas, ticks, or lice) can be picked up from other dogs, a walk in the woods, or even in the park. Contact your vet about the best dips, shampoos, and/or oral medication suitable for the age and condition of your dog.

Years ago, heartworm infestation was confined to Southern states but with the growth of the dog population and its

"All this stick chewing just wears me out!" A Nylabone™ would be a great alternative.

Life's a beach for this Rottweiler.

mobility it has turned up just about everywhere. Your puppy won't have it at eight weeks so if you live in a warm climate or it is the mosquito season in a cold climate, your pup should be started on heartworm preventative medication. Up here in the land of ice and snow, come spring we have our dogs tested for heartworm and put them on the medication through the fall, or until the mosquito season is over. Heartworm is transmitted by a mosquito, not just any old mosquito but a special heartworm-transporting mosquito that can breed everywhere, it seems.

Rodsden's Leo of Lindenwood, CD, TT and Foxbriar's Cy vom Leo, CD. Owners, Tom Horton and Bobby Ontiveros.

It must seem to you by now that a dog can get an awful lot of diseases. But don't worry, most dogs never get any of them. Basically, the Rottweiler is a fairly healthy breed. Please don't become a dog-hypochondriac. Even dogs have "dog days," when they seem to want to just lie around and do nothing. If serious symptoms do appear, remember your first call is to your vet, not your breeder.

BLOAT

A condition that deserves special mention is bloat. Deep-chested dogs seem to be more prone to the condition and that includes the Rottweiler. Bloat causes the stomach to swell and twist and can be fatal if not attended to immediately. The remedy is surgical. And while you should only call your veterinarian in the middle of the night with dire emergencies, bloat is a dire emergency!

Proper diet for your dog should consist of a good commercial dog food as his basic diet. The dog food companies have spent much money developing the very best diet for dogs; don't mess it up with

An overweight Rottweiler may want to consider a diet soda, just for the taste of it.

"people food." They have scientifically balanced their food; don't unbalance it. Dogs require a different diet than people and if they get used to people food they might then not eat their dog food. That can produce many problems for the dog and for you, not the least of which is a stool problem. Puppies can benefit from the crunch factor in dry food and can eat it without

Bevers Fleetwood Mac hiking on the Portage Glacier in Alaska. Owner, Chuck Bevers.

making a mess. Residue and leftovers do not spoil or smell and it makes traveling with your puppy or dog ever so much easier.

We recommend three feedings a day, which makes housebreaking easier because it establishes a regular schedule for bowel movements. Dogs usually need to relieve themselves after eating, so if you feed on schedule you can get them outside on schedule. Housebreaking comes much easier when you can praise them for doing it outside rather than being upset when they do it inside. Generally speaking, within a few months the puppy will lose interest in one of the three feedings and by five months will probably be ready for two meals a day, morning and evening. He should have access to fresh water at all times, which is particularly important when you are using dry feed. Many feel that it is best to feed the adult dog a couple of meals a day rather than one large meal, as with smaller feedings there is less chance of bloat.

A/C Ch. Rodsden's Elko Kastanienbaum, CDX, TD, Can. CD. Owned by Rodsden's Rottweilers.

Don't do anything to accelerate your Rottweiler puppy's natural growth pattern. Don't overfeed him and let him get fat. Overnutrition during the growth months can alter the growing pattern and cause serious bone and joint abnormalities. Feed him a normal, well-balanced diet; a good commercial dog food is your best source. Aim for average growth, not maximum growth! This is especially important in this breed, as Rottweilers are a fast-growing but slow maturing breed. A Rottweiler looks his very best at age three to five years mature in body and mind.

LYME DISEASE

One species of tick, *Ixodes dammini,* the tiny deer tick, is the culprit which transmits the germ that causes Lyme disease to humans and animals. Deer ticks are found on mammals and birds, as well as in grasses, trees and shrubs. They are rarely visible because they are so small (as minute as the dot above an i), but the damage they can cause is magnified many times their size.

Lyme disease can damage the joints, kidneys, heart, brain and immune system in canines and humans. Symptoms can include a rash, fever, lameness, fatigue, nausea, aching body and personality change among others. Left untreated, the disease can lead to arthritis, deafness, blindness, miscarriages and birth defects, heart

Select Ch. Boss v d Biestse Hoeve, SchH III, IPO III, BH, CD, TD, CGC. Owner, Ken Hemmerich.

Ch. Susan Hoeve Cor Unum, CD. Owner, Sue Rademacher.

disease and paralysis. It may prove to be fatal.

People should cover themselves with protective clothing while outdoors to prevent bites. Repellents are helpful for both dogs and humans. Examine the body after excursions and see a doctor if symptoms appear.

SKIN DISORDERS

Dogs, just like people, can suffer from allergies. While people most often have respiratory symptoms, dogs usually exhibit their allergies through itching, scratching, chewing or licking their irritated skin. These irritations often lead to angry, weeping "hot" spots.

Allergies are easy to detect but difficult to treat. Medications and topical substances can be useful, in addition to avoidance of the irritant, if possible.

Since Rottweilers love to be outdoors, extra care should be taken to prevent flea and tick infestation.

CERF/OFA/VWD CERTIFICATION

Good breeders want to produce healthy, sound animals. The best way to do this is to start with healthy, normal animals judged to be free of hereditary conditions which can cause lameness, blindness and other disorders.

In the early years of dog shows, when symptoms of disease appeared, owners asked the opinion of experienced local breeders and veterinarians. As time went on, more specifics were learned about these various diseases and their heritability. Veterinarians took x-rays, performed blood tests and diagnosed symptoms. Now we are fortunate to have experts in various areas. Due to their specialized training and the numbers of cases these experts see, they are more likely to be accurate. Some have formed organizations which register clear animals and certify dogs free of hereditary disease.

Probably the first organization of its type, the Orthopedic Foundation for Animals (OFA) certifies dogs free of hip dysplasia upon clearance of an x-ray by three board-certified radiologists. Dogs must be two years old for lifetime certification. The OFA

BISS, Ch. Rodsden's Kane v Forstwald, CD. Owners, J. Klem and E. Thompson. MRC Hall of Fame, ARC Gold Producer.

Rottweiler and pals pose for a holiday portrait.

also reads and gives opinions of radiographs with evidence of other heritable bone disorders such as craniomandibular osteopathy (CMO), osteochondritis dessicans (OCD), ununited anchoneal process, Legg-Perthes disease and fragmented chronoid process. The organization's address is OFA, 2300 Nifong Blvd., Columbia, MO 65201.

Eye problems can be detected by veterinary opthalmologists available at teaching hospitals, private specialty practices (in larger cities) and at eye-screening clinics hosted by kennel clubs. These specialists examine for cataracts, entropion, pannus, retinal dysplasia, luxated lens, progressive retinal atrophy (PRA), central progressive retinal atrophy, Collie eye anomaly and other hereditary eye conditions. The Canine Eye Registration Foundation (CERF) may be contacted at CERF Veterinary Medicine Data Program, South Campus Courts, Bldg. C., Purdue University, West Lafayette, IN 47907. The age of the dog at first testing depends a great deal on the

Rottweilers can learn to tolerate and even enjoy the company of other breeds. Rodsden's Arno v Gasto and a Miniature Pinscher.

breed and the specific area of concern. A few diseases are apparent in puppyhood. CERF requires annual examination for certification of freedom from some diseases.

The Rottweiler is a breed for all seasons!

Von Willebrand's disease (VWD) is a bleeding disorder, similar to hemophilia. Clinical signs include lameness, aching joints, bloody stools, chronic bloody ear infections or a failure of the blood to clot. A blood test measures for adequate concentration of a specific clotting factor. Although it may be conducted in puppies as young as seven weeks, it should not be done within one month of vaccination; therefore, most are five or six months old. If a dog is in heat, has just whelped a litter or has been on antibiotics, the test should also be postponed for one month. Other disorders that are limited to just one or two breeds also have specific tests. Blood samples can be sent by your veterinarian to Dr. Jean Dodds, Veterinary Hematology Laboratory, Wadsworth Center for Laboratories and Research, NY State Dept. of Health, PO Box 509, Albany, NY 12201-0509.

Before you breed, determine whether or not your dog is free of these and other hereditary diseases. Although the tests involve some cost, they are not as expensive as attempting to replace faulty pups. And they are certainly much less costly than a

Rottweiler with a kissing cousin.

Rottweilers love to play ball, and a little game of fetch is the ultimate reward for a good training session.

broken heart or a damaged reputation.

BONE DISEASE

Many canine bone diseases have gained nicknames—albeit not affectionate—due to the unwieldy medical terminology. For instance, canine cervical vertebral malformation/ malarticulation syndrome is referred to as "wobbler" syndrome; panosteitis is shortened to pano; and canine hip dysplasia is often simply called CHD. The first symptom is usually a limp. Diagnosis is made through a radiograph of the affected area.

Craniomandibular osteopathy (CMO)

affects the growth of bone in the lower jaw, causing severe pain. Spondylosis is the technical name for spinal arthritis.

Hip dysplasia is a poor fit of the hip joint into the socket, which causes erosion. Wobbler syndrome affects the neck vertebrae, causing weakness in the hindquarters and eventually the forequarters. Osteochondrosis dissecans (OCD) affects joints, most often the shoulder, elbow or stifle. Ununited anchoneal process, commonly referred to as elbow dysplasia, is a failure of the growth line to close, thereby

A/C Ch. Van Tielmans Cisco CD catches a Frisbee at Brookfield Zoo's Animals in Action program. Handler, Frank Brader.

creating a loose piece in the joint. Kneecaps which pop out of the proper position are diagnosed as luxating patellas. Legg-Perthes, most often seen in small breeds, is a collapsing of the hip joint. They all result in the same thing: pain, lameness and, left untreated, arthritis.

The exception is pano, which is a temporary affliction causing discomfort during youth. Pano may be visible on x-rays, showing up as a cloudiness in the bone marrow in the long bones, particularly in fast-growing breeds.

EYES

Entropion is a condition in which the eyelid rolls inward.

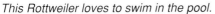

This Rottweiler loves to swim in the pool.

A very fine Rottweiler showing a handsome head.

Eyelashes rub and irritate the cornea. In ectropion, the lower eyelid sags outward, allowing dirt to catch in the exposed sensitive area and irritate the eye. In addition, extra eyelashes grow inside the lid which rub the surface of the eye and cause tearing. Either can be treated topically or, if severe, surgically.

ORGANIC DISEASE

Heart disease affects canines much as it does humans. A dog suffering from a problem involving the heart may exhibit weakness, fainting, difficult breathing, a persistent cough, loss of appetite, abdominal swelling due to fluid retention, exhaustion following normal exercise, or even heart failure and sudden death. Upon examination, an abnormal heart rhythm or sound or electrical potential might be detected, or changes in speed or strength noticed.

Treatment includes first stabilizing any underlying condition, followed by medications, low-sodium diet, exercise restriction and, possibly, surgery.

Regular exercise is essential to a healthy Rottweiler. After Schutzhund training sessions, the reward is to play Frisbee!

The best Christmas present? A big Christmas hug from their owner.

Chronic renal disease may first show up in vague symptoms—lethargy, diarrhea, anemia, weight loss and lack of appetite—as well as increased thirst and urination. Kidney disease is more common among geriatric canines. It may be compensated to some extent through diet. Diagnosis is most often made through blood and urine tests.

AUTO-IMMUNE DISEASES

Auto-immune disease, like cancer,

is an umbrella term that includes many diseases of similar origin but showing different symptoms. Literally, the body's immune system views one of its own organs or tissues as foreign and launches an attack on it. Symptoms depend on which system is the target.

For instance, hypothyroidism symptoms can include lethargy, musty odor, temperament change, decreased fertility or unexplained weight gain, in addition to the more suggestive thin dry hair, scaliness of the skin, and thickness and darkening of the skin.

Testing for hypothyroidism (which can be from causes other than auto-immune disease) may be conducted as early as eight to twelve months, using the complete blood count,

Rottweilers take a break during training.

blood chemistry, thyroid T4, T3 and free T4 tests.

Rheumatoid arthritis is a result of an auto-immune reaction to the joint surfaces. The resulting inflammation and swelling causes painful deformed joints. If the red blood cells are perceived as foreign invaders and destroyed, the rapid onset anemia (called auto-immune hemolytic anemia) can cause collapse and death if diagnosis and treatment are not quickly initiated. Often an auto-immune reaction in an organ causes destruction of that organ with subsequent loss of function. Auto-immune disease of the adrenal gland leads to hypoadrenocorticism (Addison's disease).

The same reaction in the thyroid gland soon has the dog exhibiting symptoms of hypothyroidism. Auto-immune diseases of the skin are called pemphigus, while those of connective tissue are termed lupus. Many other varieties exist, and each requires

Beautiful depiction of a Rottweiler at rest.

Ride 'em cowboy! A Pomeranian gets ready for a ride at the Rottweiler rodeo.

specialized testing and biopsy. Most respond to treatment once a diagnosis is made.

EPILEPSY

Probably because of the feeling of helplessness, one of the most frightening situations a dog owner can face is watching a beloved dog suffer seizures. As in people, epilepsy is a neurological condition which may be controlled by anticonvulsant drugs.

Many breeds of dogs have a hereditary form of epilepsy usually with an adult onset.

The University of Pennsylvania Canine Epilepsy Service has conducted studies of drugs and dosages, their efficacy and long-term side effects, to assist veterinarians in prescribing anticonvulsants.

ALTERNATIVE TECHNIQUES

During the 1970s and '80s, acupuncture, chiropractic and holistic medicine became part of the canine health picture. Veterinarians who have received special

Rottweilers stopping to smell the roses after a tiptoe through the tulips. Breeder, Linda Latham. Photo by Isabelle Francais.

treatments. Patients have responded favorably to these methods, especially when done in conjunction with medical supervision. Certainly, when it comes to a much-loved animal, the most recent up-to-date techniques should be tried before resorting to euthanasia.

Owners should be aware, however, that practitioners must have a veterinary degree to practice on animals and that the holistic, chiropractic and acupunctural treatment should not take the place of standard veterinary medicine, but enhance it.

training in these fields now practice their techniques on patients who do not respond to or cannot take previously prescribed medical

GERIATRICS

As dogs age, problems are more likely to occur, just as they do in their human counterparts. It is even more important to examine your dogs, noting every "normal" lump and sag, so that if a new one occurs you are aware. Owners should make appointments for veterinary check-ups at least once a year.

Elderly canines suffer the same infirmities as we do when we age. Deafness, arthritis, cancers, organ disease and loss of vision are common. Symptoms such as a cough, bloating, weight loss, increased water consumption and a dry thin coat are warning signs to seek medical attention. Many aging patients can be made

Schutzhund obedience...the retrieve over the 6 ft. scaling wall.

An adorable photograph of a potentially dangerous moment. Children, dogs, and pools don't mix without adult supervision.

comfortable and sustain a quality life.

Although our dogs will never live long enough to satisfy us, we can extend their lives through our precautions, specialized nutrition, exercise and routine veterinary care.

EMERGENCIES

The get-your-vet-on-the-phone-drive-there-as-quickly-as-is-safe emergency situations are few, thankfully. But they do occur, and that's why all owners should be aware of symptoms. Veterinarian numbers for day and night calls should be posted prominently near the phone.

Occasions that are well worth a middle-of-the-night payment are: shock, anoxia (choking), dystocia (labor and whelping complications), hemorrhage, gastric torsion, electric shock, large wounds, compound fractures and heat stroke. In addition, neurological symptoms such as paralysis, convulsions and unconsciousness indicate an emergency. If your dog has ingested poison, been severely burned or hit by a car, for instance, call an emergency number for help.

EUTHANASIA

Most owners dread facing the decision of euthanizing a pet. But as hard as it is to make that decision and drive a beloved animal on his final journey, it is more difficult to watch a dog who has lost all quality of life struggle through a day-to-day fog of pain. Of course, it's also more stressful for the animal, and don't we love him enough to spare him that trauma? Certainly, eyes that plead "Help me" deserve a humane response.

Euthanasia is a fact that most breeders and pet owners must eventually face if they do not wish their

This Rottweiler displays clear healthy eyes.

animals to suffer. Ask your veterinarian to administer a non-lethal anesthetic or tranquilizer, literally putting the dog to sleep while you hold your pet and caress him gently. The dog will drift off to sleep peacefully and without fear, no longer suffering. At that point, the veterinarian injects a lethal overdose of anesthesia which instantly stops the heart. Death truly comes as a servant in peace; euthanasia is a kind, quiet death.

Arrangements should be made for the disposition of the body prior to the euthanasia. Some owners wish to bury the remains themselves (be aware of local regulations, however, which are becoming more stringent) or to have

Rottweiler finally closes the deal with a lovely businesswoman.

Strong, adaptive, and intelligent, the Rottweiler makes a great companion.

the dog cremated. Others want the veterinarian to handle the arrangements. Planning ahead saves more difficult decisions during the trauma of losing your friend.

VETERINARY SPECIALISTS

With a surplus of small animal veterinarians expected in the latter part of the 20th century, and a surging volume of knowledge and medical technology, many veterinary school graduates elect to specialize with additional courses and training. These include surgery, dentistry, oncology, radiology, neurology, cardiology, dermatology, ophthalmology, theriogenology (reproduction) and internal medicine.

This "overpopulation," naturally, is a boon to pet lovers. If your dog has one of these problems, your veterinarian may refer you to a board-certified specialist or contact one for advice on specialized treatment. Any concerned, caring veterinarian will be happy to do so and assist his patient to live a healthier, fuller life.

Everyone who owns dogs for very long

An adorable group of Rottweilers pose in their little red wagon.

begins to build a canine medical chest. Basic supplies should include cotton, gauze, tweezer, ipecac, muzzle, styptic powder, cotton swabs, rectal thermometer, petroleum jelly, hydrogen peroxide, ear medication, anti-diarrhea preparation, ibuprofin pain killer and one-inch adhesive tape. Include first aid instructions and a poison help sheet with a hotline number.

ETHICS

In all diseases, symptoms may vary from mild to severe. In the most extreme cases, victims may have to be euthanized. Many do live, however, under veterinary care and supervision, occasional medication and owner TLC. Nevertheless, it's important to know which disease are known to be inherited. Our dogs can carry the factors which transmit hereditary conditions and pass on their afflictions to a higher than normal percentage of their progeny. Affected dogs should be spayed or neutered and never allowed to transmit their discomfort to future generations. Owners should also be aware that AKC regulations specify that surgically corrected dogs may not compete in the breed ring.

Good dog health care consists of commonsense and a list which should include:

1. Proper diet.

2. Clean, roomy housing and a place of his own (crate, dog run, your guest room).

3. Daily exercise and work (which for a Rottweiler is training).

4. Regular check-ups by your vet.

5. Minimal grooming.

6. And of course, love and companionship.

A pair of pups left by the Easter Bunny.

Calm, confident, and courageous, the Rottweiler will become the dog you train him to be.

Rottweilers as Support Dogs

Following in the pawsteps of the other service organizations, training schools now offer a method of independence to people who are confined to wheelchairs or who need assistance because of other physical limitations. Canine candidates for this service are acclimated to wheelchairs and crutches. Instructors teach dogs to open doors, push elevator buttons, pull wheelchairs up ramps, or act as support for a person climbing stairs.

Saddlebags are often part of the support dog uniform. Owners fill them with a purse, shopping purchases or school books.

Because of the physical assistance needed by some owners, support dogs must be strong and large enough to carry out the necessary tasks. Obviously, a toy breed could not support the weight of a grown man attempting to rise from a chair. But if the only requirement is for the dog to act as a companion and bring the owner his wallet or

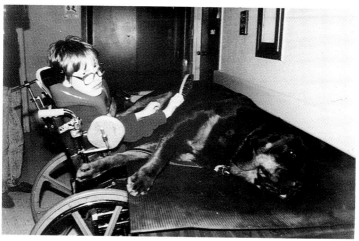

Rottweilers are welcomed at hospitals and nursing homes all over the country as Therapy Dogs.

glasses, a toy might do just fine.

Support dogs probably receive more individualized training than any of the other service dogs. This is because each person has very different needs and limitations. A busy working person who is confined to a wheelchair may demand more physical exertion from his dog than would a youngster or one who is at home a great deal of the time. Owners who walk appreciate the comfort of knowing that help is always available to lend assistance with heavy doors, to give support when climbing stairs or

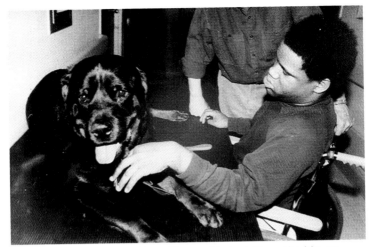

The Rottweiler's patient disposition and trainability make him an ideal Therapy Dog.

to retrieve a dropped object.

Owners find that a dog bolsters confidence through aiding independence and by offering protection. Animals often smooth the way to new friendships by serving as a conversation ice-breaker. Also, canine companions—unlike humans—are always willing to fetch and carry without grumbling or resenting that they're overworked. In addition, a support dog sometimes actually strengthens the owner by requiring the person to exercise otherwise unused muscles.

The Rottweiler's intelligence and versatility allow him to serve in several different capacities as a support dog.

SUPPORT DOG ORGANIZATIONS

People who wish to find help or make a donation to a support organization can contact the following:

Aid Dogs for the Handicapped
1312 Bergan Road
Oreland, PA 19075
215-233-2722

Canine Companions for Independence
P.O. Box 446
Santa Rosa, CA 95402-0446
707-528-0830 (V/TDD)

Canine Working Companions
RD 2, Box 170
Waterville, NY 13480

315-861-5215 (TDD)

Dogs for Independence
P.O. Box 965
Ellensburg, WA 98926
509-925-4535

Freedom Service Dogs, Inc.
980 Everett Street
Lakewood, CO 80215
303-234-9512

The Companion Dog Connection, Inc.
3865 Minnehaha Avenue South
Minneapolis, MN 55406
612-729-5986

Helping Paws of Minnesota, Inc.
P.O. Box 12532
New Brighton, MN

55112
612-924-2404
**New England
Assistance Dog
Service**
P.O. Box 213
West Boyleston, MA
01583
508-835-3304
Paws With a Cause
1235 100th Street
S.E.
Byron Center, MI
49315
616-698-0688
(V/TDD)
**Phydeaux's for
Freedom, Inc.**
1 Main Street
Laurel, MD 20707
301-498-6779
**Responsible Pet
Ownership**
3624 Fisher Road
Palm Harbor, FL

34683
813-787-5433
**Southeastern
Assistance Dogs
The Speech, Hearing
and Learning
Center, Inc.**
811 Pendleton Street
9-11 Medical Court
Greenville, SC 29601
803-235-9689
803-235-6065 (TTD)
**Support Dogs for
the Handicapped,
Inc**.
P.O. Box 966
St. Louis, MO 63044
314-487-2004
314-739-3317
**Wisconsin Academy
for Graduate Service
Dogs**
Rt. 1, Box 139
Janesville, WI 53546
608-752-3990

References

"EFFECTS OF EARLY EXPERIENCES ON DEVELOPMENT OF DOGS" lecture by Dr. Ferdinand Brunner of Vienna at the Fourth Congress of the International Federation of Rottweiler-friends, 1978.

HOW TO RAISE AND TRAIN A ROTTWEILER, 1964, Joan R. Klem and P. G. Rademacher.

UNDERSTANDING YOUR DOG , by Dr. Michael W. Fox.

THE NEW KNOWLEDGE OF DOG BEHAVIOR by Clarence Pfaffenberger.

HOW TO RAISE A PUPPY YOU CAN LIVE WITH Rutherford and Neil.

"LETS TALK ABOUT ROTTWEILERS" Video, JK Video Concepts, Joan R. Klem.

SPECIAL THANKS TO:

THE MEDALLION
ROTTWEILER CLUB
    Carol Krickeberg, Pres.
    4469 Little Rock Rd.,
    Plano, IL 60545

THE COLONIAL
ROTTWEILER CLUB
    Anthony Di Cicco, Pres.
    10 Oceanview Rd.
    Lynbrook, N.Y. 11563

THE GOLDEN STATE
ROTTWEILER CLUB
    Deborah McIntyre, Pres.
    15 Santa Clara Street
    Laguna Hills, CA 92656

THE AMERICAN
ROTTWEILER CLUB
    Catherine Thompson, Pres.
    47 Yellowbrook Rd.
    Freehold, NJ 07728

INDEX

More Rottweiler Books from T.F.H.

TS-147, 446 pages. Over 700 full-color photographs.

H-1083, 336 pages. Over 575 full-color photos,

H-1035, 544 pages. Over 85 full-color photos.

PS-820, 256 pages. Over 100 full-color and black and white photos.

All-Breed Books from T.F.H. Publications, Inc.

KW-227, 96 pp. 100 color photos.

SK-044, 64 pp. Over 50 color photos.

TW-113, 256 pp. 200 color photos.

H-1061, 608 pp. 100 B&W photos.

TS-101, 192 pp. Over 100 photos.

H-1016, 224 pp. 135 photos.

H-1091, 912 pp.
Over 1100 color photos.

TS-175, 896 pp.
Over 1300 color photos.

TS-220, 64 pp.

TS-205, 156 pp.
Over 130 color photos.

H-1106, 544pp.
Over 400 color photos.

TS-212, 256 pp.
Over 140 color photos.

TS-220, 64 pp.